THE MAKING OF SCOTLAND

**Philip Gaskell and
Arnott T Wilson**

Designed and illustrated by
Sydney McK Glen

Cover design by
Hilary McElderry

Holmes McDougall Limited, Edinburgh

Contents

Acknowledgements

The authors and publishers are grateful to the following for permission to reproduce copyright material:

Front cover, the Gundestrup Cauldron, reproduced by kind permission of the National Museum of Denmark; Glasgow Art Gallery & Museum, pages 3 (top right), 8 (bottom right), 9 (middle & bottom right), 25 (top right); reproduced by kind permission of the Society of Antiquaries of Scotland, pages 3 (middle right), 13 (bottom right) from volume 86 of the Society's Proceedings, 24 (top right), 26 (top right); National Museum of Antiquities of Scotland, pages 3 (bottom right), 6 (middle right), 7 (middle right), 8 (top right), 9 (top right), 10, 11 (top and middle right), 13 (top and middle right), 14 (middle left), 15 (bottom left), 19, 21 (middle right), 25 (two middle right), 27 (top right), 28 (bottom left & right), 29 (top left & right), 32, 35 (right); Hunterian Museum, pages 4 (top), 14 (right), 15 (top left), 17 (bottom); Crown copyright: reproduced by permission of the Department of the Environment, pages 5 (middle left), 7 (top left, right, bottom left), 12 (top left), 15 (middle right), 18 (bottom right), 21 (bottom right), 22 (top left), 24 (top left), 25 (two bottom right), 31 (bottom left), 36 (bottom right), 39 (bottom left); R. Feacham, *Guide to Prehistoric Scotland*, Batsford Publishers, page 5 (top right); Miss I. J. McInnes, page 6 (top right); A. S. Henshall, *Chambered Tombs of Scotland*, Edinburgh University Press page 6 (bottom right); Euan Mackie, *Scotland an Archaeological Guide*, Faber and Faber, pages 7 (bottom right), 24 (middle left), 27 (middle), 30 (top right & bottom), 45 (bottom right); after Stuart Piggott, page 8 (middle); Banff Museum, reproduced by courtesy of North-East of Scotland Library Service Museums Service, page 12 (bottom right) Royal Commission on Ancient and Historical Monuments of Scotland, page 12 (top right); Cambridge University Collection: copyright reserved, pages 14 (bottom left), 39 (top left); S. Frere, *Britannia*, Routledge & Kegan Paul, page 16: Crown Copyright — reproduced with permission of the Controller of Her Majesty's Stationery Office, page 17 (top left); G. Menzies, *Who are the Scots?*, B.B.C. Publications, pages 18 (left), 22 (middle right); Dean and Chapter of Westminster, page 26 (bottom left); Museum of Islay Life, page 31 (top right); *An Historical Atlas of Scotland c.400-c.1600,* eds Peter McNeill & Ranald Nicholson with the permission of the Trustees of the Conference of Scottish Medievalists, pages 33, 35 (left), 41; Copyright University Museum of National Antiquities, Oslo, page 34; Mansell Collection, pages 38 (bottom left), 46 (middle).

Published by Holmes McDougall Ltd
Allander House
137-141 Leith Walk
Edinburgh EH6 8NS
Copyright © 1979 Philip Gaskell and Arnott T Wilson
SBN 7157 1834-7

The First Peoples

The hunters

Think about a land where everything was covered in ice and snow, all year round. This land was Scotland, 10 000 years ago.

Very slowly the ice began to melt away so that plants were able to grow and animals could find food further and further north. Following the animals, the first people came to northern Britain over 7 000 years ago.

- Why did the people follow the animals north?
- Which areas of Britain would they have come from?

Archaeologists have uncovered *evidence* which helps us understand how they lived. They have *excavated* rubbish piles, including whale bones and shells, left by the first peoples which show that they must have hunted animals, gathered plants and berries and caught fish. To help catch and prepare food the people used stone weapons and tools.

- Why do you think the people ate these foods?
- Draw some of the tools and describe how they could be used.

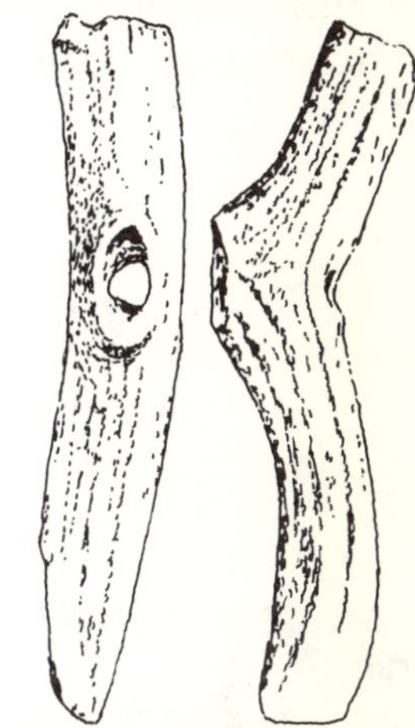

Shell midden (rubbish pile)

Hunters returning with food for the family

Two views of an axe made from reindeer antlers, found in Stirlingshire

Some sharp flint arrowheads and tools

A boat hollowed out from the trunk of a tree

The hunter people were *nomads*, never staying in one place for long. Most of the *middens* have been found close to the sea, on both the East and West coasts. Archaeologists believe that the first peoples fished from small boats hollowed out of tree trunks, some of which have been found buried near rivers. One of these boats has been found buried under layers of clay which were laid down over 7 000 years ago.

- What would make the people move to a different part of the country?
- Do you think that the first peoples would have been able to harpoon whales and catch them from their boats? If not, how can you explain the discovery of whale bones in their rubbish piles?
- What else could the people have used boats for, apart from fishing?
- From the evidence you have seen, write a description of daily life for the first peoples in northern Britain.
- How can archaeologists tell the age of the objects they find?

The farmers

Around 3 500 years *B.C.* (5 500 years ago) a new group of people gradually made their way northwards and brought with them a different way of life. The archaeologists have called them the farmers, as these people cleared the land and planted *cereal* crops. The farmers did not move around like the hunters, but settled on their farms.

- Why does the planting of crops show us that the farmers had a different way of life from the hunters?

Some of the farmers also kept animals, like pigs or cattle, which could be fattened and killed for food. The bones which archaeologists have found from this time are often the

Farming people planting seed on cleared ground and herding domestic animals

bones of young animals. This probably means they were slaughtered every autumn, so that the people had enough meat to last through the winter.

● How do you think they stopped their meat rotting through the long winter months?

On the mainland archaeologists have not been able to find the remains of these first farmers' houses, which, we assume, must usually have been made from wood. The wooden buildings would have collapsed and rotted. But the village of Skara Brae in Orkney, where there are few trees, was built of stone and the houses have survived. The buildings and *artifacts* found at Skara Brae give us a good picture of the farmers' daily lives.

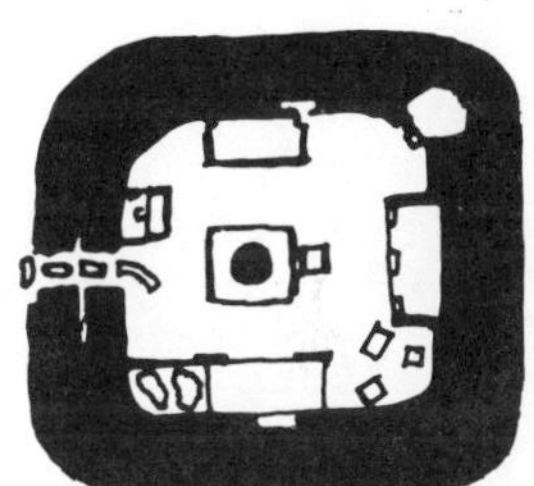
A plan of one of the stone houses at Skara Brae

The inside of one of the houses at Skara Brae

The evidence shows that, like us, they had ovens, sideboards, seats and beds, but theirs were made of stone. In the floor of some of the huts there were clay lined pits which may have been filled with cold water, so that fish and other food could be kept fresh.

● How many of these everyday things can you see in the photograph or plan?
● The oven is not shown in the illustrations. What do you think the oven would have looked like and what would have provided heat for it?

On this page you will see examples of the pottery left behind by the farmers, which they would use to prepare or store food or perhaps other objects.

- Using this pottery as your evidence, how do you think you can show that the farmers were not nomads?

Scientists can *analyse* old stones to find out which area they came from, and from the evidence of stones and stone tools found on the sites of early *settlements* archaeologists are sure that the villages in different areas were trading with each other. The farmers had learned which were the best varieties of stone for making their axes, scrapers and other tools. To get these good stones they traded with other parts of the country where these stones were found and made into tools.

- Can you think what the farmers might have exchanged for the stones?
- Here you can see some illustrations of stone tools. Can you think where handles might have been attached to the axe heads? What would the handles have been made of and why have they not survived?

Although most of the first farmers' houses have not survived, their tombs have, because they were built of stone. From the excavations which have been made so far, it is possible to draw a map to show where these tombs are found.

- What does this tell us about the farmers? Would they have lived far from their burial grounds?

You can see that some of the tombs are clustered together in some areas. Some of the tombs are huge structures which must have taken a long time to build. The farmers must have organised themselves to carry out the work, but we do not know how this was done. The tombs may well have been *communal*, as a small group of people, who may even have been priests, were buried in them.

- Who do *you* think was chosen to be buried in these tombs? Why?

Apart from telling us where the farmers lived and that they were able to organise people to build them, the tombs also shows us that the farmers had some sort of religion, although we cannot tell what this was. Below, you will see pictures of carved stone balls which may have been used as charms to help chase away evil forces. Another idea is that they might have been used for some sort of game. Sometimes tombs are found inside stone circles or beside stand-

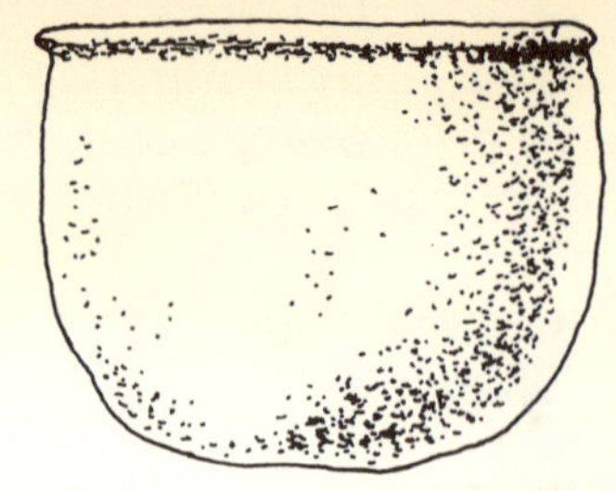

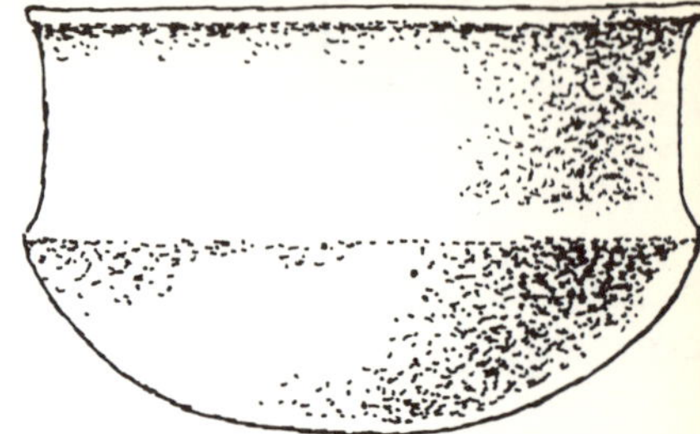

Pieces of pottery from Fife and Midlothian, left by the farmers

Stone axes found in Argyll, Shetland, Dundee and Lanarkshire

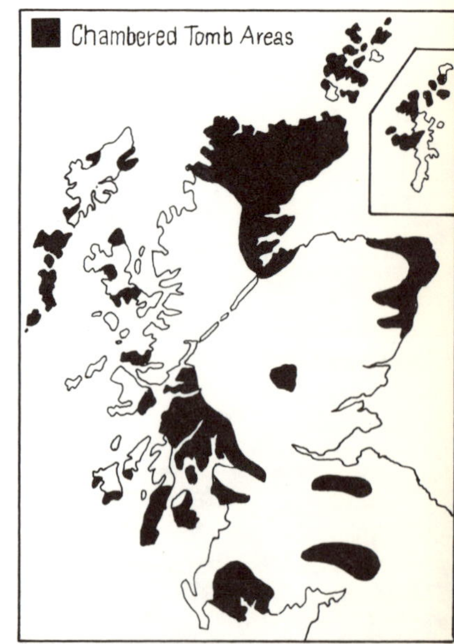

This map shows where chambered tombs have been found in Scotland

ing stones. So we think the farmers' religion was probably connected with these mysterious standing stones and circles, which were built about 2 500 B.C. (4 500 years ago).

Some of the circles, as you can see, have been found to be exact circles and ellipses. Some archaeologists think that the stones themselves were *aligned* with hills or mountain peaks where the sun or moon would have passed, either rising or setting, at midsummer or midwinter, thousands of years ago.

- Why would it have been important for the people to know when midsummer or midwinter was approaching?

Some archaeologists also think that the people had a *system of measurement* which enabled them to build these perfect circles. Many of the 'cup and ring' marks which were probably made by farmer people on carvings and rocks have been found in northern Britain. Others think that the artifacts, particularly the pottery, of the farmers were too clumsy to have been made by people who had an accurate system of measurement. Instead they believe that the circles were used only at magical or *ritual* meetings, and were not deliberately lined up with peaks in the distance.

- What do you think the purpose of the standing stones and stone circles was from the evidence so far?

Above left: A tomb at Camster, Caithness

Above right: A tomb at Maes Howe, Orkney

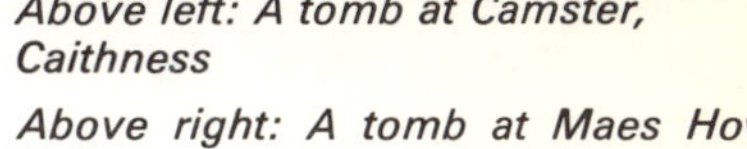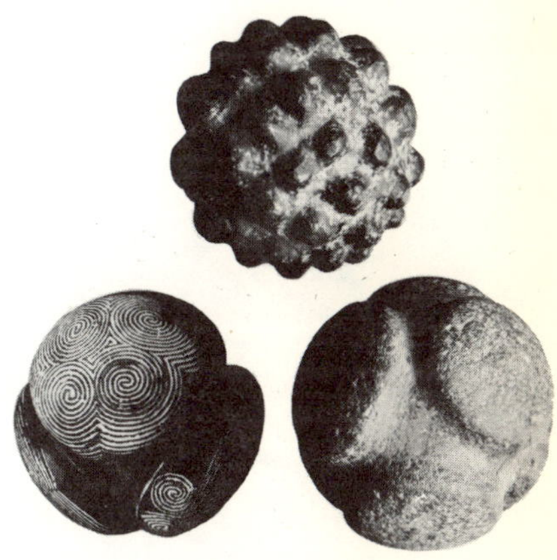

Some carved stone balls left by farmers

Left: The Standing Stones of Callanish, Isle of Lewis

A plan of Burgh Hill, a stone circle in Roxburghshire

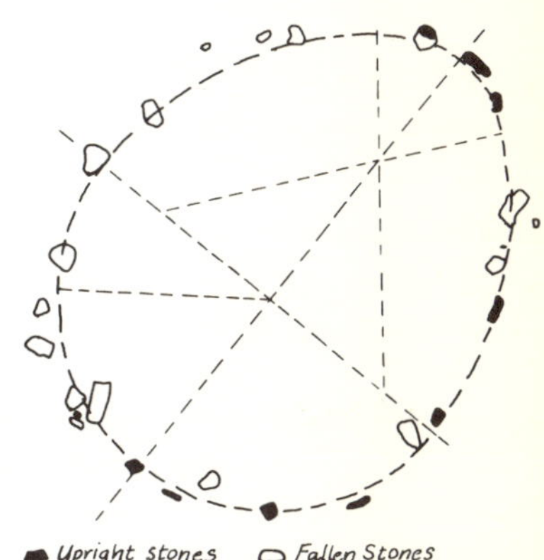

The Beaker people

About 2 000 B.C. (4 000 years ago) the farmers were disturbed by the arrival of a new group from the continent. Archaeologists have called the newcomers 'Beaker people' because the shape of the pottery which they used is something like a beaker. This pottery has often been found as *grave goods* buried with their bodies. When the skeletons of the Beaker people were compared with those of the farmers, it was found that they were a little taller than the farmers and had broader faces and shorter skulls.

- What do you think the 'Beaker' pots were used for?
- Why do you think grave goods were buried with the bodies?
- What does the difference between the skeletons of the Beaker people and the farmers tell you about the two groups?

One of the Beaker people's pots

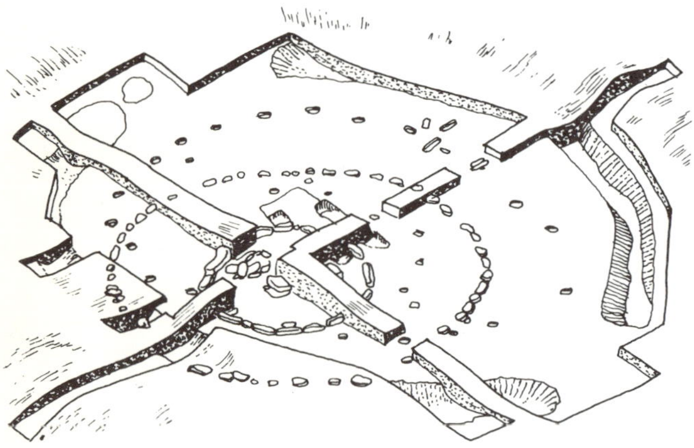

A plan of Cairnpapple Hill where the grave of a Beaker chief was found

At Cairnpapple Hill in West Lothian a Beaker chief was buried in a grave surrounded by standing stones and the earlier graves of farmers. Excavations of the graves show that the farmers were cremated first and the ashes of many of them were then buried in the same grave. The Beaker man was buried by himself with two Beaker pots and a wooden club beside him.

- Why do you think the Beaker people buried their dead this way?

Bronze spearhead and axehead found in Renfrewshire

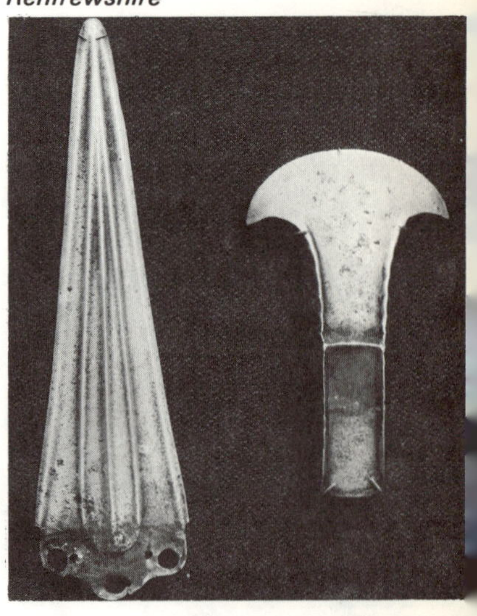

The Beaker people were *metalworkers* who had found out that by melting down copper and tin and mixing them together in stone moulds, they could produce much better tools and weapons made of *bronze.*

- What might the large number of bronze weapons which have been found mean about the way the people lived?
- Why do you think the farmers had not found out about the metalworking process themselves?

By this time the people were certainly in contact with and traded with other groups like themselves in southern Britain and perhaps even on the continent. As their metalworking skills increased they produced things like razors, small blades, axes, chisels, knife-blades and weapons such as swords, spearheads and dirks. Even some of the metal-working tools, like hammerheads and anvils, have survived in a few places. People became more skilful in making objects from bronze. They learned how to make the socketed axehead.

- Why do you think the socketed axes were easier to use than the older axes?
- What difference do you think these metal artifacts made to everyday life?

The other examples of the metalworkers' *craft* which have survived are beautiful gold and silver necklaces and bracelets. You can see an illustration of one of these below.

As time passed the farmer and Beaker people mingled, developing new skills but living much the same sort of life over a very long period of time. The way they buried their dead shows how the ways of life of these two different peoples became mixed together. They now burned their dead and put the ashes in special urns or pots which they sometimes buried in tombs not unlike those of the early farmers. Most of the urns, though, were buried in single flat graves.

The *population* lived in the same areas, probably in the same kind of villages, farming the land in a way which really lasted until the last century, when farming became much better organised.

- What sort of skills and knowledge did the first peoples pass on to their children?
- In what ways is rural life in Scotland different today?

More questions and assignments

1   Copy down the list below into your jotter and then write in the meaning for each of the words. Use the word-list on page 48 and a dictionary. Add other words that you don't know to the list and find out their meanings too.

    Evidence   Radioactivity   Grave Goods   Bronze
    Excavate   Archaeologist

2   Imagine that you are with a group of the very first people to come to Scotland 7 000 years ago. Tell the story of one day and what your group did. Remember that most of the day would be spent finding food and protection and shelter for the night.

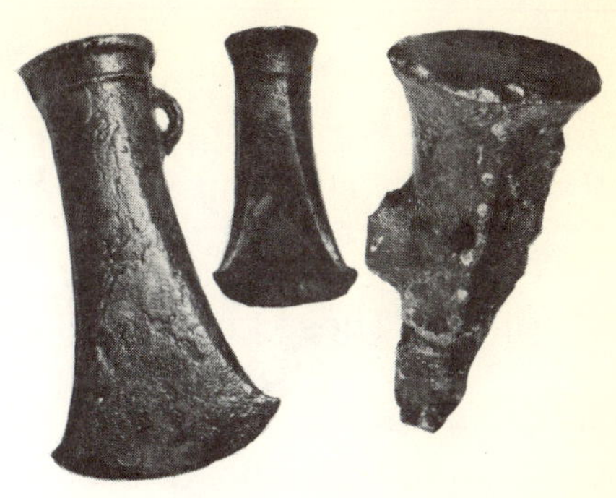

A bronze socketed axe, an anvil and a gouge

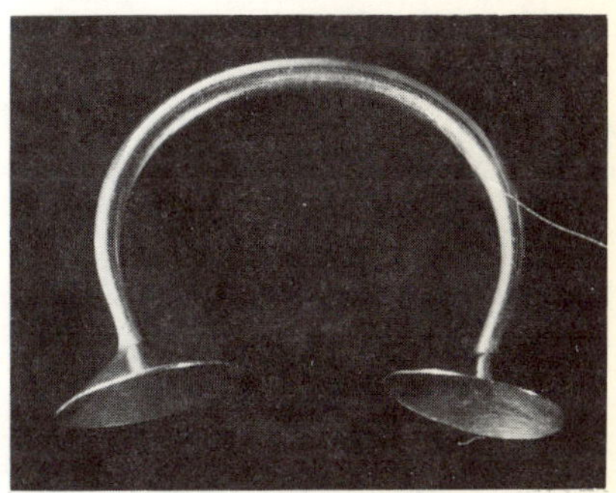

A gold necklet from Arran

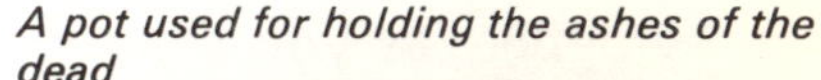

A pot used for holding the ashes of the dead

2

The Celts

Most of the people called Celts began to arrive in northern Britain from Germany about 700 - 800 years B.C. (2 700 - 2 800 years ago) but some arrived much earlier than this. They must have come in different groups because linguists can tell that they spoke two separate kinds of the Celtic language. These languages are still spoken today as Gaelic in some parts of Scotland and Ireland and as Welsh in Wales, though some of the words and spellings have changed.

This is how an explorer from Carthage, called Himilco, who lived about 500 B.C., described the Celts:

The people who inhabit the islands are proud and skilful workers who trade on routes along ranges of hills and sail far and wide through the wild sea in boats which they so skilfully make from skins bound together.

Another writer, Poseidonius, who lived about 100 B.C., tells us:

They gather their corn harvest by cutting off the ears only and store them in underground pits . . . Both men and women wear gold ornaments, massive gold collars and remarkable rings of pure gold. They are tall and have soft white skin, their hair is naturally blond, but they make it lighter by artificial means and to make it shine they often wash it in a lotion of lime.

Some Celtic ornaments: a bronze bracelet, necklace and mirror and a bone comb

Archaeologists have found objects which back up the written evidence, as you can see from the pictures.

● What does the existence of mirrors tell us about the Celts?

Later the Celts were able to work in iron as well as in bronze and gold and used their skills to improve the *implements* being used by the farmers and traders already living in Scotland.

The Celts were a warlike people, even fighting against each other. Poseidonius describes them like this:

When quarrels break out between them they challenge each other to single combat. In making war, they use two horse chariots which seat a driver and a warrior. When they attack an enemy a spear is thrown first, then the warrior dismounts and fights with his sword. They cut off the heads of defeated enemies and preserve them in the oil of the cedar tree and proudly show them to strangers.

Iron axe and some smith's tools (a hammer and tongs) found in a grave in Islay

The archaeological evidence also gives us a warlike picture of the Celts. Stone-walled hillforts were first built about 800 B.C. probably at the time of the main Celtic arrivals. Some of the stone walls of the fort had a wooden frame. Timber-lacing was a skilful technique also in use in Germany. It was used to steady and strengthen the loose rubble core of the wall. Some of the stones in the walls of the hillforts have been found *vitrified* or fused together. This may have been the result of a fire-raising enemy attack, or perhaps just an accidental fire.

- How do you think we know that the Celts were warlike?
- How do we know that the timber-lacing technique was used in Germany?

Hillforts have been excavated mainly in the south and east of Scotland, for example at Traprain Law, near Haddington. In the same areas, people also lived in settlements which were *palisaded.* Walls of earth and ditches were also put round these villages in later times, and these walls and ditches can sometimes still be seen. At Dreva Craig, near Selkirk, rows of stones were driven into the ground in front of the first wall.

- Why do you think these sites were surrounded by wooden fences?
- What do you think the stones in the ground were there for, bearing in mind that the Celts probably had horse-drawn chariots?

Inside the settlements the remains of timber huts have been found, like those in the drawing above. Some written evidence from Poseidonius survives which describes the way the Celts lived:

Their houses which are built of reeds and wood are simple and not at all grand.

Iron spearheads and boltheads found in Roxburghshire

Bronze horsebits from Dumfries

Left: Dreva Craig

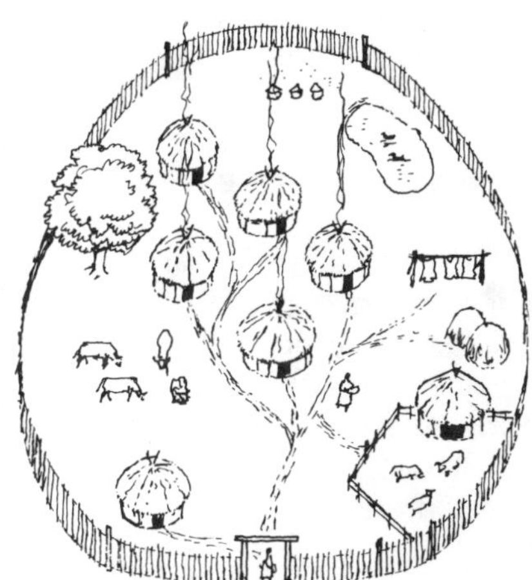

A drawing to show what a palisaded settlement probably looked like

A drawing of a vitrified wall

The broch on the Island of Mousa

Dun Aisgain, Mull

In the north and west people lived in different kinds of places called *duns* and *brochs.* These usually took up much less space than the forts. Duns were round or D-shaped and had walls of stone. The brochs, which probably came later, usually had double walls of stone with stairs between the walls. Some of the brochs were very tall and one on the island of Mousa in Shetland is still over twelve metres high.

- From the evidence so far, do you think the Celts changed the way of life of the earlier settlers?

By the time of the birth of Jesus (over 1 900 years ago), different groups of Celts lived in different parts of the country, each *tribe* occupying a particular area. We do not know very much about how these tribes were organised, but if you look at the written evidence from Poseidonius who lived until 50 B.C. you will get some idea of who had power among the Celts:

The island of Britain is heavily populated and several kings and chiefs rule its different areas. The nobles shave their cheeks but allow their moustaches to grow and cover the mouth. When they eat, they do not sit on benches but squat on wolf and dog skins on the ground . . . Their dress is very strange; their tunics are dyed in many colours, and they wear a patterned cloak fastened at the shoulder with a brooch. In battle they carry a shield as tall as a man, each warrior decorates his own shield sometimes with animal shapes made of bronze. Their metal helmets are ornamented with large projections, like horns, which make the warrior look tremendously tall. Strange shaped trumpets which make hoarse warlike sounds are used to spread terror among the enemy. Their swords are double-edged and hang from their sides by chains. Some warriors carry pikes with iron tips, 50 cm long.

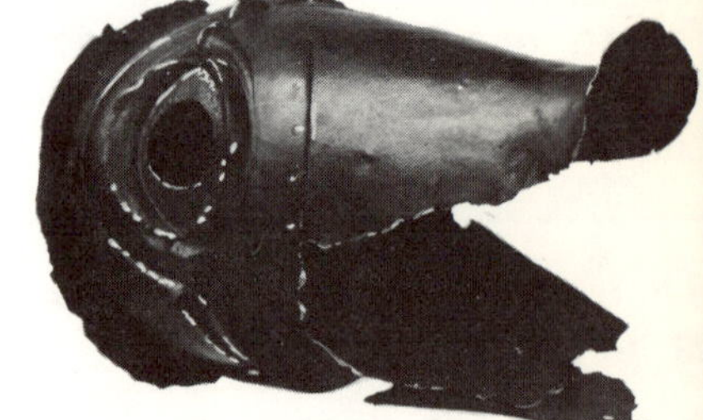

A bronze trumpet made in the shape of a boar's head

- Do you think that the evidence in the illustrations in this chapter supports what the writer says?

The Celts probably had an organised religion with some sort of priests. Poseidonius describes them like this:

There are also philosophers and prophets who are treated with great respect and honour; these prophets foretell the future from watching the flights of birds and from inspecting the insides of sacrificed animals. These men have great power in times of peace and war.

A three-faced, carved stone head

Archaeologists have found some carved stone heads which may have had something to do with their religion.

- Give your own ideas about what part these heads might have played in the Celtic religion.
- Why do you think the Celts were important in the "Making of Scotland"?
- What, if anything, introduced by the Celts survives in Scotland today?

More questions and assignments

1. What did the Greek traveller Poseidonius say about the Celts?
   Write down what he tells us about their way of fighting and make drawings of the weapons he tells us about — you will find pictures of these on page 11.
2. Copy these sentences into your jotter and fill in the missing words:
   "The Celts made weapons and tools from . . . and . . . . They liked to look fine and wore ornaments made of . . . . They stored their corn in . . . . Boats were made from . . . fastened together."
3. Make a drawing of a broch. Write three lines to describe how the broch is built.
4. What have you found out about Celtic religion and how the Celts tried to foretell the future? Write five lines describing the Celtic religion.
5. Make a list of all the words you don't know the meaning of in this chapter. Find out the meanings and write them out.

A piece of checked woven material dating from the mid-third century, discovered at Falkirk

Diagram of what the material would have looked like when it was new

3

The Romans

The next invaders of the lands which are now Scotland were the Romans, who in the first century *A.D.* (about 1 900 years ago) controlled nearly the whole of Europe from their capital city at Rome in Italy. Unlike the Celts before them, the Romans were concerned with extending their *empire*. The Roman army moved northwards to expand their *province* of Britannia and to control the warring tribes of Celts who were invading this province.

- How would the *influence* of the Romans be different from the influence of earlier invaders?
- Where do you think the province of Britannia was?

A Roman milestone from Bridgeness, Bo'ness, showing on the left invading Roman soldiers

A model of a Roman soldier

Most of the Romans who lived in northern Britain were soldiers. Wherever they went, the Romans built camps and forts. Archaeologists can show us where the Romans went and what their life was like by finding and excavating ruined buildings and objects left by them. Sometimes archaeologists use *aerial photographs* to find Roman camp sites which are difficult to see on the ground.

An aerial photograph of a Roman fort in Dumfries

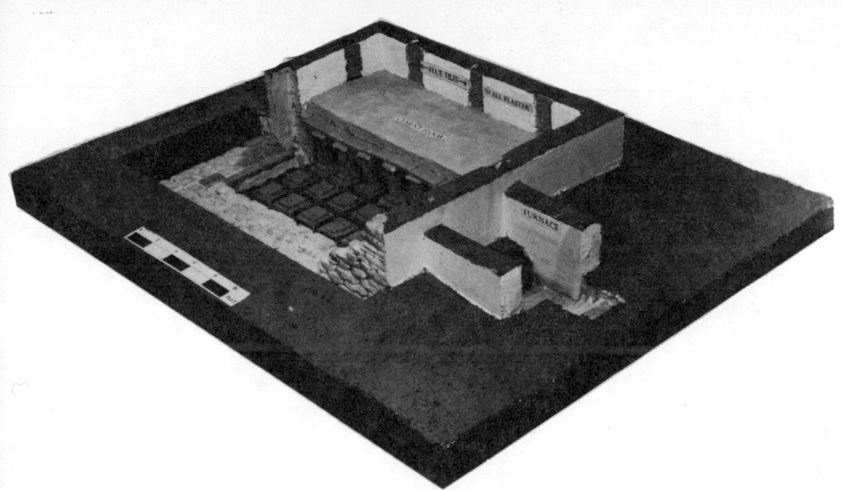

A model of a hypocaust

- On this page you can see a picture of a *hypocaust*. Find out what this was and how it worked. What is its modern name?
- What sort of game does the one shown on the sandstone block in the picture remind you of?
- Find out about life in Rome. How did it differ from the life of Roman soldiers in northern Britain?

We know about the organisation of the Roman army from the writings of many authors. Tacitus, who lived from 57-120 A.D., wrote the story of Agricola's campaigns in Britain. This is especially important for us. Tacitus often mentioned soldiers of different ranks in his descriptions of the Roman army. Apart from this written evidence, we know how the Romans organised themselves from pictures carved in stone showing the army in action. (Trajan's column in Rome shows many battle scenes.)

A gaming board carved out of sandstone

Three Roman legionaries from a gravestone in Dunbartonshire

Agricola, who built Inchtuthil fort, was the first Roman leader to fight against the Celtic peoples. He marched northwards, first conquering the tribes living in the southern parts of what is now Scotland. This is an account of his *campaign* by Tacitus:

In his third year of campaigning in Britain, Agricola conquered all the tribes who live to the south of the river Taus and in the next year he succeeded in controlling the narrow neck of land between the Clota and Bodotria which are two rivers that almost cut the land in two. Having won many battles against tribes which before that time had not been known to the Romans, Agricola and his armies moved north again.

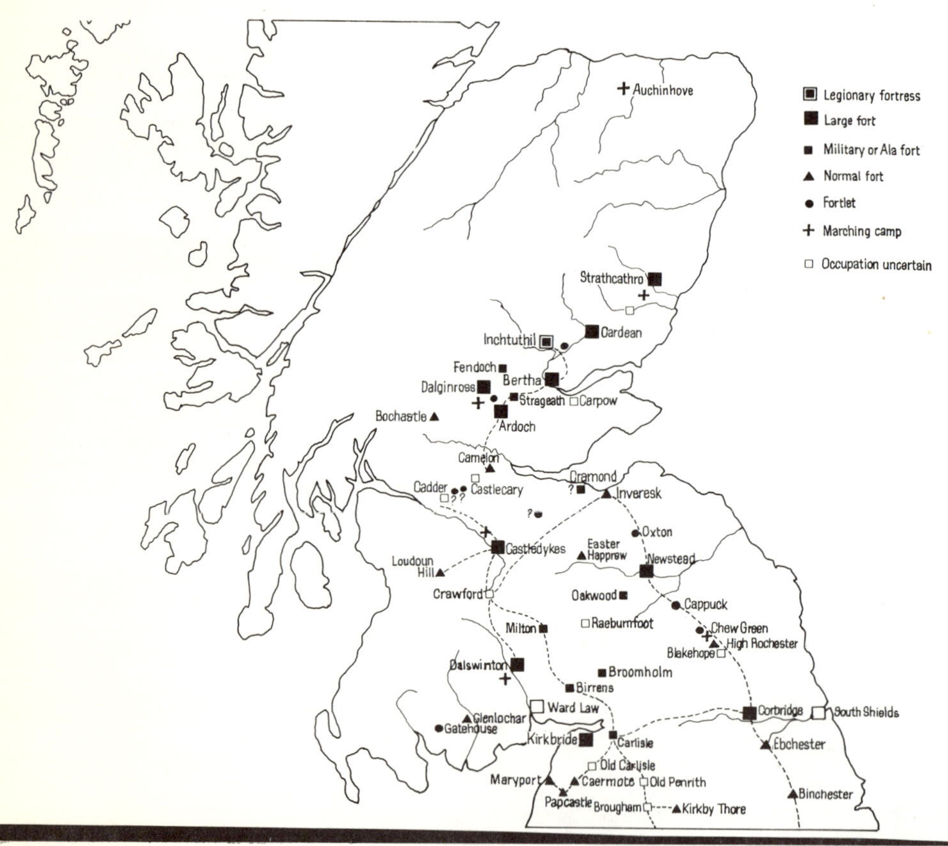

This map shows the main settlements in Northern Britain under Agricola

- Which big rivers do you think Tacitus meant when he wrote about the Clota, the Bodotria and the Taus?
- Tacitus was Agricola's son-in-law. How does the fact alter your belief in what he writes?

Look at the map which shows Agricola's control of Scotland. As you can see he built many forts and roads in *strategic* places.

- Why do you think the Romans built forts in these places?

Cuddys Crag, Housteads Fort on Hadrian's Wall

Agricola had fought and won battles, the most important being Mons Graupius, but had difficulty in ruling the native tribes. The "Life of Hadrian", written between 300 and 400 A.D., tells us that in 121 A.D. the Emperor Hadrian was the first to build a wall eighty miles long to separate the *barbarians* from the Romans.

This wall, known as Hadrian's Wall, was built across what is now northern England, and parts of it can still be seen today. It must have looked very big and strong to peoples like the Selgovae, the Novantae and the Brigantes, with its wall forts every mile and huge ditches to the north and south.

● Why do you think the Romans built ditches to the north *and* south of Hadrian's Wall?

The Romans managed to control the tribes of the south-west by building more forts and roads. But more trouble from the northern tribes meant that the Romans had to build another wall, to keep these tribes in their northern lands. This wall was called the Antonine Wall, and parts of this too can be seen today. A writer called Capitolinus, who wrote near the end of the third century, describes the events which took place about 140 A.D.:

Antoninus Pius conquered the Britons through Lollius Urbicus the governor, and after driving back the barbarians, built another wall, this time of turf . . .

● Find out exactly where the Romans built these walls.

This model of a section of the Antonine Wall shows the ditch dug in front of the wall for greater protection

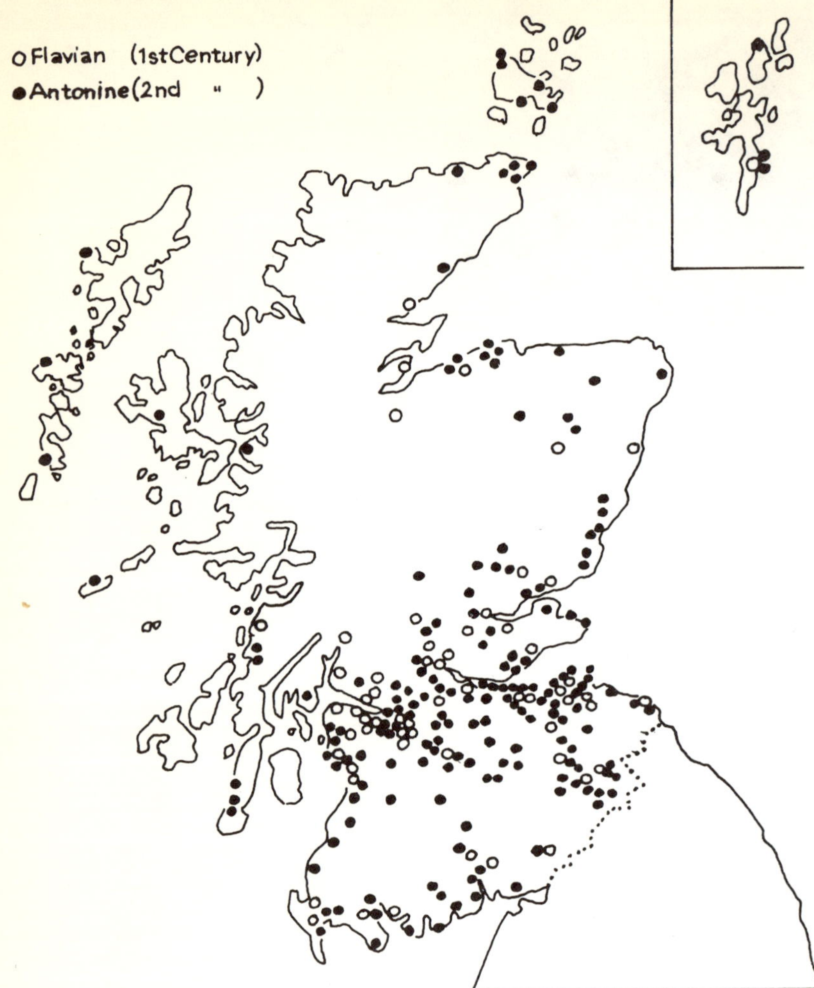

This map shows the places where Roman objects were found in areas not lived in by the Romans

A head of Fortuna, one of the Roman goddesses

Probably some of the peoples south of the Antonine Wall would have become friendly with the Romans. It may be that the Roman coins and other objects found at places where the native people lived show that the Romans and natives traded with each other.

Many Roman stones have been found with writing on them about gods and goddesses, like Apollo, Minerva and Jupiter, who the Romans thought, controlled everything from great victories to the weather.

- Can you think what the native peoples might have traded in return for the Roman coins and objects? (Remember that the Romans were mainly soldiers.)
- How does the evidence about the Roman religion differ from the evidence of the religion of earlier peoples?

Roman writers like Dio Cassius and Herodian tell us that the fighting in northern Britain went on until about 200 A.D. The Emperor Severus decided to subdue the Caledonians and the Maeatae, the two tribes of the north. Severus had a difficult campaign and did not manage to control the northern lands for long.

The Romans really thought of Hadrian's Wall as the *frontier* of Britannia, and just tried to prevent the Celtic tribes from invading their province. But after about 300 A.D. the Romans grew much weaker and in about 400 A.D. they abandoned Hadrian's Wall as they withdrew to the south, leaving the lands of the north.

- What did the Romans leave the natives with?
- How much of their influence has survived today?

More questions and assignments

1   Draw a map showing Agricola's route through Scotland. Write 5 lines to explain how archaeologists found out which places Agricola's army went to.
2   Find out how the Romans built their roads.
3   Find out more about Trajan's column in Rome. Draw some scenes from the carvings on it.
4   Draw a Roman soldier like the one on page 14 and put labels on the drawing to show the following pieces of equipment: sword, helmet, shield, sandals, metal breastplate, leather tunic, spear.
5   Imagine that you are a Roman soldier on guard duty on the Antonine Wall. Write a letter to your family telling them about your life in northern Britain. Be sure to mention your daily duties, food, weather, the Celtic peoples and their way of life.
6   Look at the Roman objects below. Explain how *you* think the Britons got hold of them. Why did they hide them?

Part of the Roman silver treasure hidden at Traprain Law

4

The Four Peoples

When the Roman armies left northern Britain, there were two peoples descended from the Celts who had been living in the land for many centuries. The Romans used the nickname Picts for the two northern tribes whose real names were the Caledonians and the Maeatae. They both lived to the north of the Antonine Wall. The other people, who lived mainly to the south of the wall, were the Britons.

But the Picts and the Britons did not have northern Britain to themselves at this time. Even before the Romans left, Scots from Ireland were invading and settling on the west coast. A monk called Bede, writing in about 730 A.D. (about 1 200 years ago), tells us about these first three peoples:

After the Britons and the Picts, Britain received a third race, the Scots, who settled in part of Pictland. They came from Ireland under the leadership of Reuda. From long ago the Britons and Picts have been separated by a great inlet of the sea which runs far inland from the west, nearby that inlet stands a very strong city of the Britons which is called Alcluith (Dumbarton). The Scots settled on the north side of the inlet.

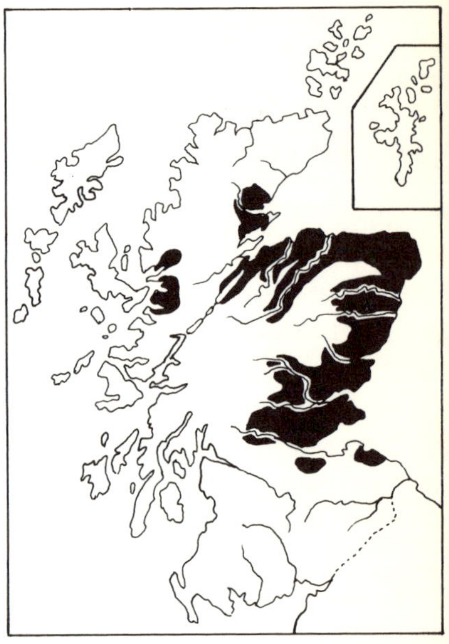

A map of places with Pictish names

● Which 'great inlet' do you think Bede had in mind?

Other early writers tell us that in the south-east the lands of the Britons were invaded by the Angles, an English speaking people who had originally come from the land which is now Denmark.

For the next few centuries these four peoples had to share northern Britain. Very often they fought each other, but very gradually they came together under the leadership of the Scottish King and so the country got its name.

Linguists can tell us the areas different peoples lived in by plotting the different names they gave to hills and other *landmarks* on a map. This evidence agrees with Bede's description.

● Draw a map of Scotland which shows clearly where the four peoples lived.

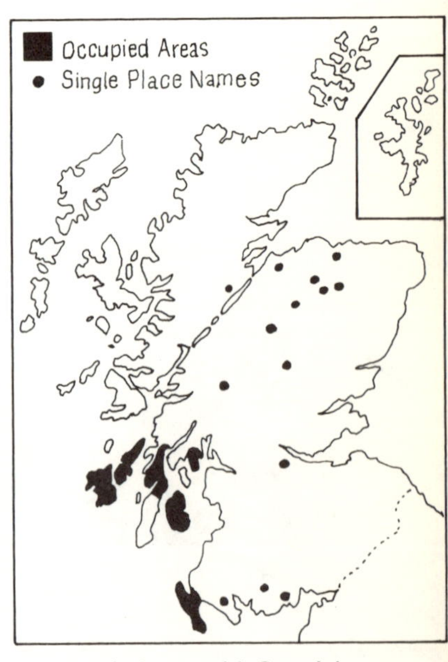

A map of places with Scottish names

The Picts

The Romans used the nickname Picts for the Caledonians probably because they painted or tattooed themselves. In Latin, the Roman language, 'Picti' means 'painted people'. We know very little about the Picts because they left no histories of their people; all that they left are lists of the names of their kings and big stones with symbols and pictures carved onto them.

But we can get some idea of how the Picts lived by looking at the histories of other peoples, and by examining what archaeologists have dug up. However, we cannot believe all the descriptions of these people. Here is a strange story about the Picts in 874 A.D. from an early "History of Norway" written not long before 1200 A.D.:

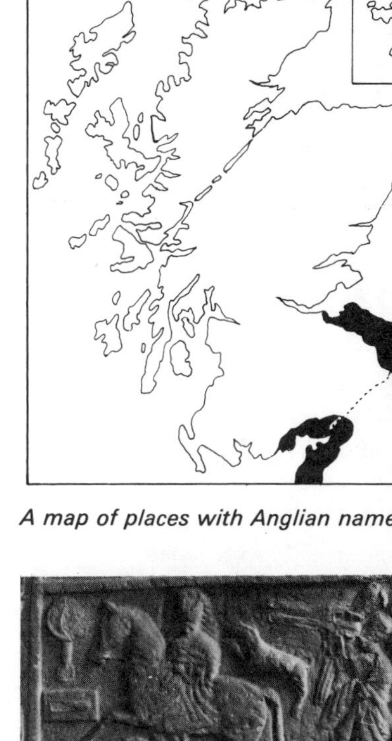
A map of places with Anglian names

The Picts were little bigger than pigmies in stature, they did marvels, in the morning and in the evening, in building walled towns, but at mid-day they entirely lost all their strength, and lurked through fear in little underground houses.

- Do you really believe that they lost all their strength at mid-day?

We know this is a *myth* because the skeletons of Picts which have been found are about the same size as ourselves.

- What does the photograph of the picture on the stone tell you about how the Picts got their food?

Unfortunately hardly any examples of Pictish houses have been found, perhaps because they were often made of wood. Remains of stone-built houses have been discovered in Orkney, and although there is not much material left,

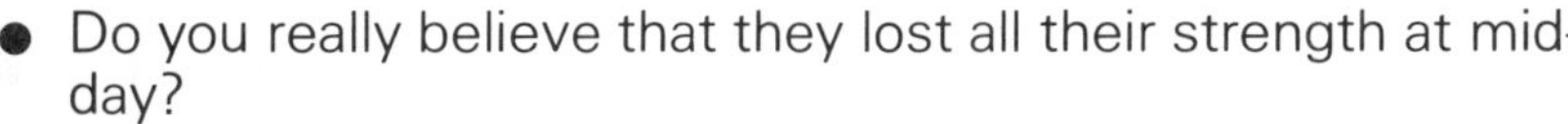

A hunting scene which was carved on stone by the Picts

Gurness in Orkney. The Picts used the stones from brochs to build their own stone houses

The remains of a pictish house at Buckquoy in Orkney

archaeologists can try to give us some idea of what the houses would have looked like.

Some of the kings of the Picts were powerful enough to make war against the Britons of the south or the invading Angles who were taking over the areas which belonged to the Britons in the east. William of Malmesbury, writing hundreds of years later, described the year 671 or 672 A.D.:

. . . when King Oswy of the Angles died the Picts saw their chance to attack the new kingdom and united together to make war against the Angles . . . But the young king destroyed the Pictish army so that a river near the battle was blocked with the dead.

- What other evidence is there in this chapter which helps to support the idea that a great deal of warfare was taking place?
- What sort of clothes did the soldiers wear and which weapons did they use? Illustrate your description.

In the year 685 A.D., the Pictish army won an important victory at Nechtansmere against King Ecgfrith of the Angles. Bede describes the battle like this:

King Ecgfrith of the Angles, against advice given to him by his friends and especially St. Cuthbert led an army to make great destruction in Pictland. The Picts pretended to retreat and led Ecgfrith's army into wild mountains which the Angles did not know. There King Ecgfrith and most of his men were killed and from that time the power of the Kingdom of the Angles began to sink, and the Scots and Picts regained the land which the Angles had conquered from them and many of the Britons also recovered their freedom.

- In this piece of evidence, what can we use to prove that the Pictish leader was a clever soldier?
- Why was Nechtansmere such an important victory for the Picts?
- On this page, you will see pictures of Pictish symbols to be found on many of their big stones. What do you think these signs could have meant?

The Picts disappear from history in the middle of the 9th century A.D. (about 850 A.D.). Nothing more is heard of them.

Pictish warriors from a section of Sueno's Stone

Some drawings of Pictish symbols

The Scots

The Scots came from Ireland and settled in an area we call Argyll and which they called Dalriada. They arrived in sailing vessels called 'curraghs' — some carried as many as 28 men, 2 on each bench.

This was probably how the King Fergus Mor, son of Erc, left Ireland and came to live in the new Dalriada a little before 500 A.D.

A curragh — the sailing vessel in which the Scots came from Ireland

Just like the Picts, the Scots had to fight to keep their new lands. Fergus Mor's great grandson, King Aedán, who reigned from 574-608 A.D., was one of the most important of the early kings of Dalriada. He won many battles in places as far apart as Orkney and the Isle of Man, but his greatest enemies were the Angles, and he was defeated by them in 603 A.D. This is how Bede describes him:

In these times a most powerful King ruled over the Angles and he was very much feared by the Britons for the damage his armies did to them. Now Aedán King of the Scots who lived in Britain was also anxious about this and attacked the King of the Angles with a great army, but Aedán was beaten and fled from the battle with only a few of his men, because almost all his army had been killed at a place called Degsastan. And never from that time has any King of Scots dared to come to battle against the Angles.

- What does Fergus's arrival tell us about the importance of the new Dalriada?
- Bede himself was an Angle. Do you think his description of the battle would have been fair?

Some archaeologists believe that Dunadd in Argyll, where the Scots had a fortress on a rocky hill top, was the capital of Dalriada for some time. As you can see from the plan, the fort itself was well defended by *ramparts*, but we know that the marshy land round about Dunadd would also have helped to protect it from attack.

● How would marshy land have helped to defend Dunadd from attackers?

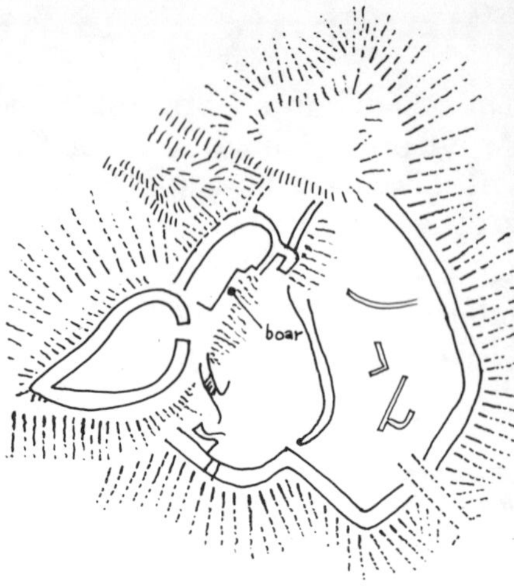

A plan of Dunadd showing the ramparts which defended it

Dunadd, Argyll, a Scottish fort which may have been the Scottish capital

Ardifuir Dun in Argyll was probably another Scottish settlement

Some of these settlers may have lived at Ardifuir dun in Argyll. As you can see it lies in a valley, and from where the photograph is taken it must have been easy to throw spears or boulders at the dun. Some may have lived in *crannogs* — houses built by earlier people in the middle of a loch.

● Can you think of any reason why some Scots may have lived at Ardifuir in a valley, bearing in mind that the Scots probably had an organised, trained army?
● Why do you think some Scots may have lived in houses on lochs?

Most of the houses which have survived were built for security against enemies, but of course many Scots would have probably lived in very simple houses made of wood near the land they farmed. There must also have been *craftsmen* who carved fine wooden ornaments and made gold jewellery.

The Scots of Dalriada had divided themselves into three main groups or 'cenéla', the Cenél Loairn, the Cenél nOengusa and the Cenél nGabráin. The ruler of each of these groups was called a *'rí'* or king, and usually one of them would also be an over-king for the whole of Dalriada. The king could be *succeeded* by some of the members of his *kin*, but usually before he died he would choose perhaps a brother, cousin or nephew to take over.

On this page you will see a photograph of a footprint and a hollowed out basin, at Dunadd in the territory of the Cenél Loairn. This probably had something to do with the 'making' of a new *'rí'* or king.

● Have you any idea why a footprint was used?

The church and especially the holy man called Columba who came from Ireland in 563 A.D. had a lot of power among the Scots. Adomnan who wrote Columba's life story about 690 A.D. says:

One day, Columba questioned King Aedán about a successor to the kingdom. When he answered that he did not know which of his three sons should reign, Columba asked to see the youngest and said, "This is the survivor, and he will reign after you as king; and his sons will reign after him." All these things were completely fulfilled afterwards in their time.

● How do you think Columba predicted this?
● Why would this make him important?

The Scots also fought against the Picts. In 741 A.D. they suffered a very heavy defeat by Oengus King of the Picts, who may have had the Pictish boar carved at Dunadd to celebrate his victory.

But from then on, the power of the Picts grew weaker. The Picts found that they had to fight the Scots in the south and the Vikings in the north. They couldn't easily fight both powerful enemies for long. A *chronicle* tells us about the events in 843 A.D.:

When Viking pirates had conquered the coastal areas and killed huge numbers of Picts who defended their lands, Kenneth MacAlpin invaded Pictland and made war against the Picts. He killed many of them and the others fled. So he was the first of the Scots to become king over the whole land which is now called *Scotia*.

A model of a crannog

The Monymusk Reliquary — a wooden box with bronze fittings for holding relics

The Hunterston brooch which was found in Ayrshire

The footprint at Dunadd

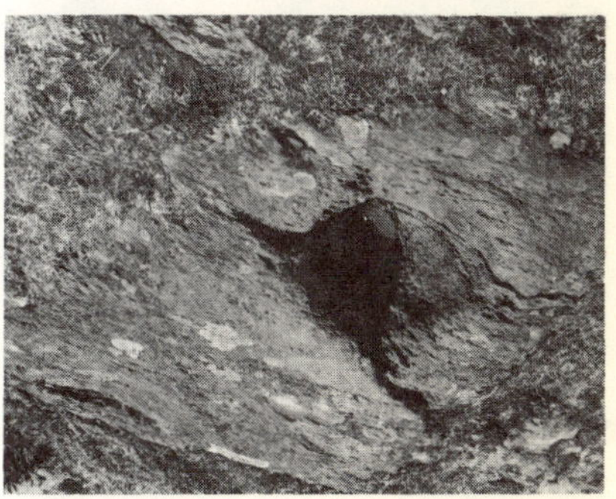

The basin at Dunadd

The land of the Picts became the land of the Scots, and the Pictish way of life was lost.

The Scots now had most of the lands north of the Forth-Clyde line.

King Kenneth made Scone the capital of the new kingdom of Scotia. The Scots claimed to have brought with them the sacred Stone of Destiny, on which they crowned all their kings.

A drawing of the Pictish boar carved at Dunadd

- Where is the Stone of Destiny now?

Almost immediately Kenneth made attacks south of the Forth against the Angles of Northumbria. One hundred years later Edinburgh was captured by the Scots and after another hundred years had passed, the whole of Lothian came under Scottish control.

Symeon of Durham, who wrote in the early part of the twelfth century (after 1100 A.D.), tells us:

In the year of the Lord's incarnation, 1018, when Cnut was King of the English, a *comet* appeared for 30 nights to the people of Northumbria. This was thought to mean that some disaster would soon take place. 30 days later at a battle fought at Carham, a huge army of Scots destroyed almost the whole Anglian army. With the King of Scots was Owen, king of the men of Strathclyde.

Only a few years later, the Scottish king, Duncan, inherited the British kingdom of Strathclyde so that the Scots had now taken over the whole land later to be known as Scotland.

The Scots' sacred Stone of Destiny

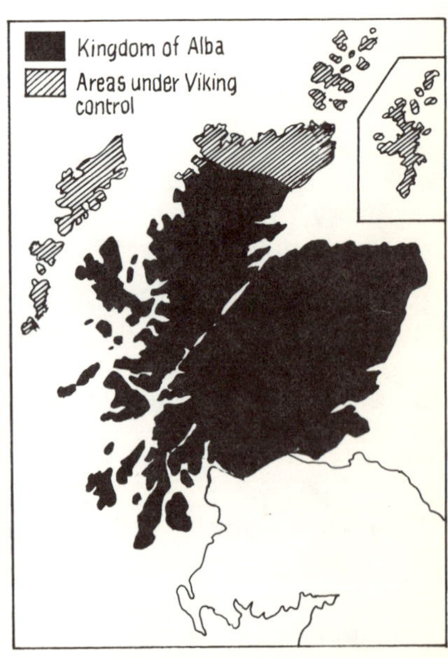

This map shows the Viking threat to the Scottish kingdom of Alba

Britons and Angles

At the time when the Romans left northern Britain, most of what is now southern Scotland was inhabited by people of the British tribes. But before long their territory was invaded by English speaking Angles who took over a lot of their land. So the British tribes were under attack from the south and east by the Angles and by the Picts and the Scots from the north. King Arthur whom we hear about in legends may have been one of the leaders of the Britons as they fought the invaders who surrounded them.

Not much evidence has survived about the British kingdom. We know that Dumbarton rock was probably one of their most important *strongholds*. It was also near the edge of the territory of the Scots.

● Why do you think the Britons chose Dumbarton rock as a stronghold?

The crosshaft of an Anglian stone from Dumfries showing the elaborate carving

Dumbarton Rock — one of the most important British strongholds

The Britons also lived in a settlement at Traprain Law. Some implements have been found there.

- What do the objects in the pictures on these pages tell you about the way of life of the Britons?

Warfare still played a big part in the way of life, even when the Angles had gained control of the British territory, as Bede tells us when he described the year 633 A.D.:

And when Edwin had ruled most gloriously for 17 years over the nations of the Angles and of the Britons, Catguollaun, king of the Britons, rebelled against him. And a severe battle was fought in the plain which is called Hatfield, and Edwin was killed. And his whole army was either killed or chased away.

Traprain Law, East Lothian, where the Britons had a settlement

A ploughshare from Berwickshire

A sickle found at Traprain Law

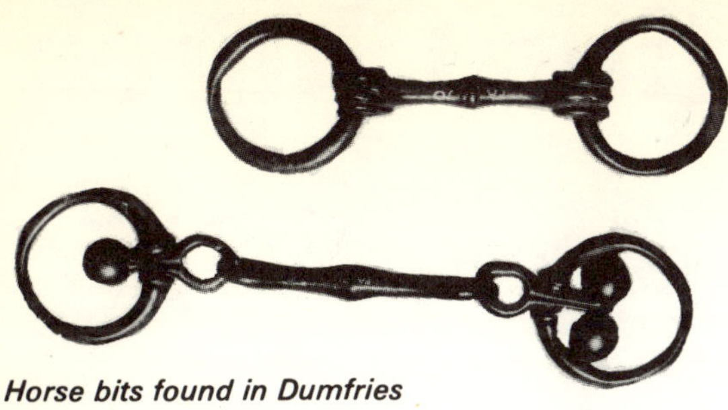

Horse bits found in Dumfries

More often though the Britons found themselves under attack and the Vikings even managed to take over Dumbarton.

The Anglian way of life must have been very similar to that of the Britons. We know a bit more about them because of the many ornamental and sculptured stones and crosses which can be seen in many areas of south and south-east Scotland today.

Because there are many good examples like those in the pictures, archaeologists think there must have been craftsmen among the Angles, as well as other groups like nobles, holy men (like Bede), lawyers, and peasants.

As you know already the areas in which the Britons and Angles lived were soon all part of the new expanding kingdom of the Scots. But the influence of the Angles especially was always very important in the southern regions of what was to become Scotland.

More questions and assignments

1 Find out the meaning of some place-names in your area.
2 What explanations can you find for the Picts 'vanishing from history' in the 9th century?
3 Draw pictures showing the different styles of decoration used by craftsmen for each of the four peoples. You will find examples of some of them in this chapter.
4 Copy down the following sentences into your jotter and fill in the missing words.
'The . . . and the . . . were in Scotland when the Romans were here. The . . . came later from Ireland, and the . . . came from northern England. The Scots called their part of the land . . ., the Kingdom of the Britons was called . . . and the Angles were in the Kingdom of Northumbria.
5 Choose three of the Pictish carved symbols and draw them. Write two lines about each one to explain what you think they mean.

An ornamental stone from East Lothian carved by Anglian craftsmen

5 The Christian Church

The Romans were probably the first people to spread the new religion. We know that in the year 313 A.D., the Emperor Constantine decided that everyone in the Empire should stop believing in the old gods and become Christians instead.

In the last chapter you read about Columba who was also important as he helped *convert* the Picts to Christianity. A long time before he lived there were other holy men, who gradually turned people away from their old beliefs. These men said it was better to be Christian, and believe only in one God.

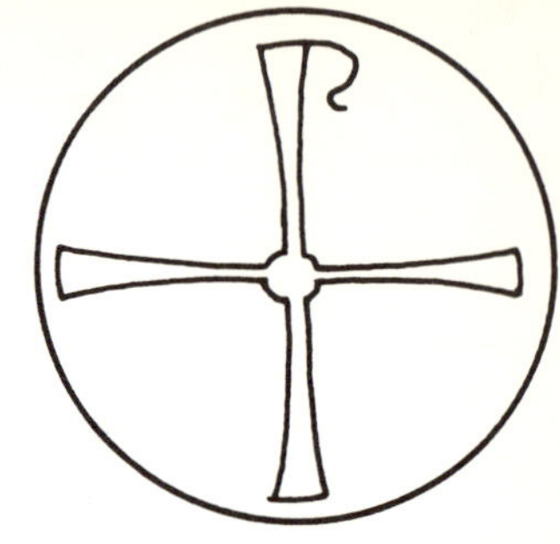

Drawings of early Christian crosses

● What shape do you notice most in the pictures on this page? Why do you think we can use it as our evidence for the Christian religion?

The first *missionary* we hear about is Ninian who was later made a saint. Bede wrote this about him:

The southern Picts who live to the South of the mountains had long before given up their *heathen* religion and accepted the true faith when the word was preached to them by Ninian, a most holy man of the race of the Britons. He built a White House, at Whithorn. This was a church of stone which was unusual among the Britons.

St Ninian's Cave

Archaeologists have found traces of an early church at Whithorn in the south west of Scotland. Christian graves, some dated between 500 and 600 A.D., have been found in Fife and Angus (the land of the Southern Picts).

The way of life of early missionaries like Ninian must have been very hard. They still had to grow crops and either hunt or keep animals for food. They must also have spent some time travelling, to convert people to the new religion. Later huge stone crosses were built, sometimes with pictures of stories from the Bible carved on them.

Bede wrote about Columba's work as a missionary. This is what he tells us:

He came to preach the word of God to the northern Picts, whose King at that time was called Brude, a most powerful ruler. Columba converted the Picts to the faith of Christ and received from them the island of Iona on which to build a monastery.

On Iona the remains of a monastery and other Early Christian buildings called cells have been found, like the ones in the pictures.

If you look at the map on page 33 in this chapter you will see where other Columban monasteries have been discovered by archaeologists. Many are in the territory of the northern Picts. One group of missionaries, the Papae, went as far north as Orkney and Shetland by land and in small boats.

Archaeologists have found remains of a monastery at the Brough of Birsay in Orkney, which would have looked something like the beehive cell in the photograph below.

The Kildalton Cross on Islay

Some beehive cells on Garvellach Isle

The Ruthwell Cross built in the eighth century

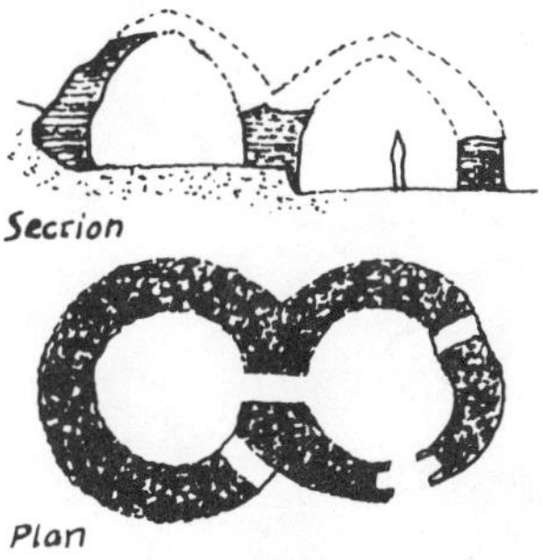

A plan and section of a beehive cell

It was probably in the eighth century A.D. (between 700 and 800 A.D.), that the St. Ninian's Isle treasure of gold and silver objects was buried in Shetland. It was uncovered again in 1958. The treasure may have been buried in the church to keep it safe from the *pagan* Viking raiders.

- Why do you think people buried their valuable objects in a church?
- Do you think the Vikings would have searched churches?

Although Columba, Ninian and their followers were all holy men, they organised their churches differently. Bede said that Ninian 'had been instructed in the mysteries of the Christian Faith in Rome'. This meant that Ninian would have been a chief priest or bishop of the Christians.

On the other hand, Bede tells us that the Columban church was different:

Iona is always ruled by an *abbot* who is in charge of a large area. He is even more powerful than the bishops. This is not the way the Roman church is organised. This practice was established by its first abbot, Columba.

Before long, the differences between the two churches became known to everyone. A special meeting, called a *Synod*, was held at Whitby around 664 A.D. King Oswy, a king of the Angles whom you heard about in the last chapter, was to decide which church his kingdom should belong to. He decided in favour of the Roman church. A few years later, both Adomnan, (the abbot of Iona who wrote about Columba) and Nechton, the King of the Picts, decided to agree with him.

But groups of priests called *Culdees* continued to live mainly in the old Columban ways for many years, although some of them were more *secular,* that is they lived more like ordinary people.

Part of the St. Ninian's Isle treasure

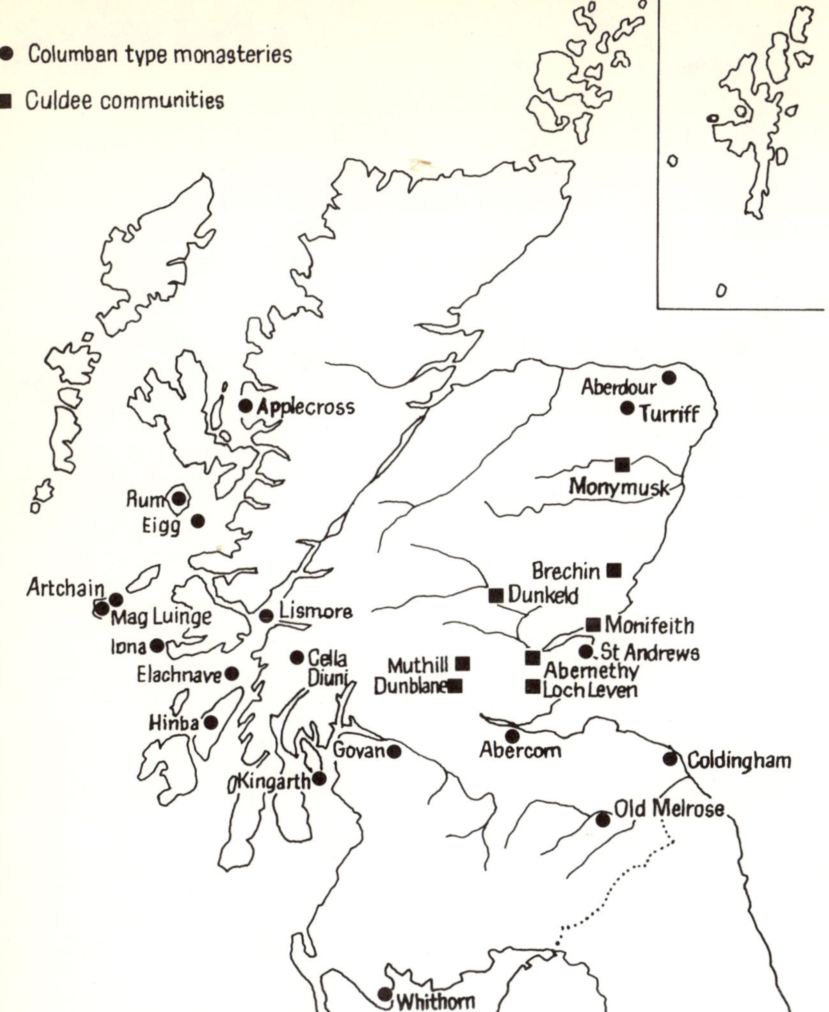

This map shows where Columban monasteries have been found in Scotland

More questions and assignments

1 Make a drawing of one of the early Christian crosses shown in this chapter.

2 Imagine that you went with St. Columba to convert the Picts. Write a report of what you have learnt about the Picts on your journey.

3 Find out the meanings of the following words and make a note of them in your jotter.

   Missionary   Preach   Convert   Monastery   Abbot Synod   Culdees   Secular

4 Make a drawing of one of these early Christian missionaries to Scotland. Find out and list the main differences between the Roman and Celtic churches. You will need to use other books to find this information.

The Vikings came by sea to Scotland from about 793 A.D. onwards, in longships. These were so well designed and reliable that fishing boats in the Faeroes are still built in the same way today. We first hear of them raiding down the west coast of Scotland.

Archaeologists have found Viking weapons, like swords, axes and shields. The Orkneyinga Saga, which is really a collection of stories about the Viking Earls of Orkney written much later in the late thirteenth century (about 1270 A.D.), describes very fierce and unruly fighters. One of the Earls was even known as Thorfinn Skullsplitter. Another Earl, who was also called Thorfinn (the Mighty), ruled from 1014 to about 1064 A.D. and sometimes fought against the kings of Scots:

Earl Thorfinn addressed his men, advising them to be smart and to make the first attack fiercely, and saying that few of the Scotsmen would be able to make a stand. The fighting was long and fierce. Arnór Jarlaskáld says, "Valiantly the Prince went forward 'gainst the King's eleven ships. All their swords were swimming in the life-blood of the Scotsmen. Hearts were sinking — bowstrings screaming; Darts were flying — spear-shafts bending; Swords were biting, blood flowed freely. And the Prince's heart was merry. Never was a battle shorter. Soon with spears it was decided. Though my lord had fewer numbers, yet he chased them all before him."

● Do you think we should trust what this saga says?

A Viking longship

Other evidence shows the Vikings were not always raiders. On this page you will see a map showing where Viking graves have been found in Scotland, and objects from one.

- Using the map say which areas of Scotland the Vikings settled in.
- What evidence tells you that Viking farmers settled here?

We know that the Vikings were interested in settling in northern Scotland, as the very first place-names which they used were for settlements in the Orkney islands. A lot of what we know about the Vikings has been learned from the writings of monks.

- Bearing this in mind, can you think of any reason to doubt the written evidence about raids and burnings?

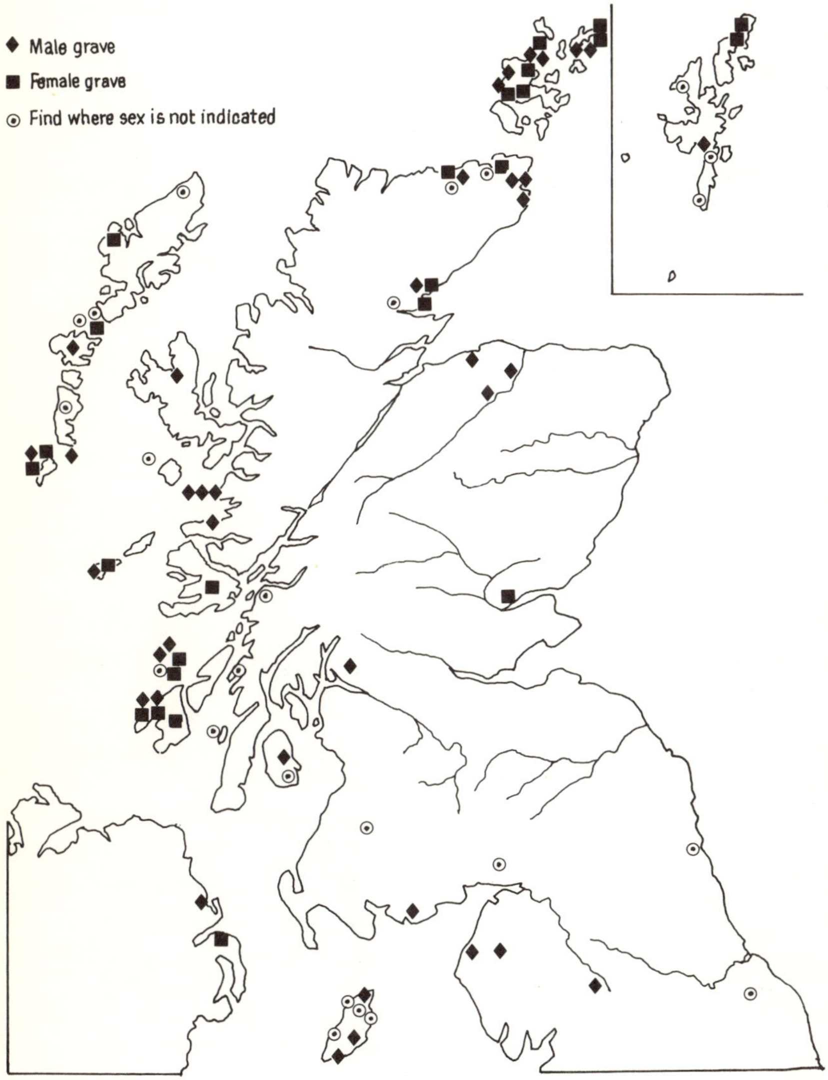

Clay objects found in a Viking grave in Shetland: a weight for a fishing line, a handled cup, a hanging lamp, a bowl and a spindle whorl

This map shows where Viking graves have been found in Scotland

There were several reasons why the Vikings came to Scotland. The evidence below will give you one reason. It comes from another collection of *sagas* called the *Heimskringla* which were told at the time of the event and written down much later. This extract describes the events of about 874 to 890 A.D.:

After a great battle, King Harald met no opposition in Norway, for all his opponents and greatest enemies were cut off. But some, and they were a great many, fled out of the country. Some Northmen went to Shetland, flying the country on account of King Harald, and went on Viking cruises into the West sea. In winter they were in the Orkney islands and Hebrides, but *marauded* in summer in Norway, and did great damage.

Fish were important to the Vikings as a source of food. So another reason for the Vikings to come to Scotland might have been a *migration* of herring away from Norway over a number of years. There may also have been too many people living in Norway, Sweden and Denmark at the time.

● What do you think was the most important reason for the Vikings coming to Scotland?

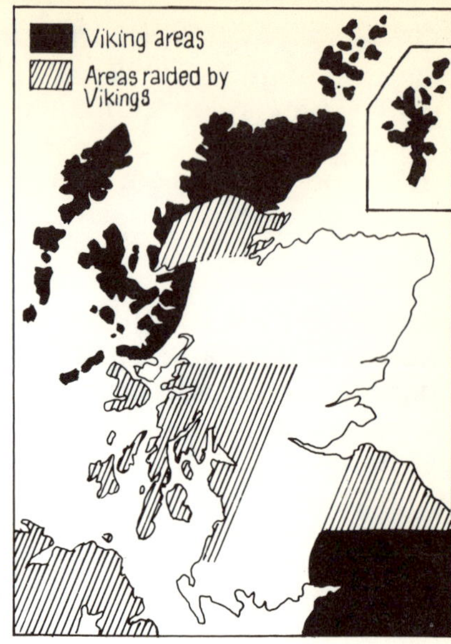

This map shows the main areas settled and those raided by the Vikings 900-950 A.D.

This is a map of the northern sea routes used by the Vikings for trade

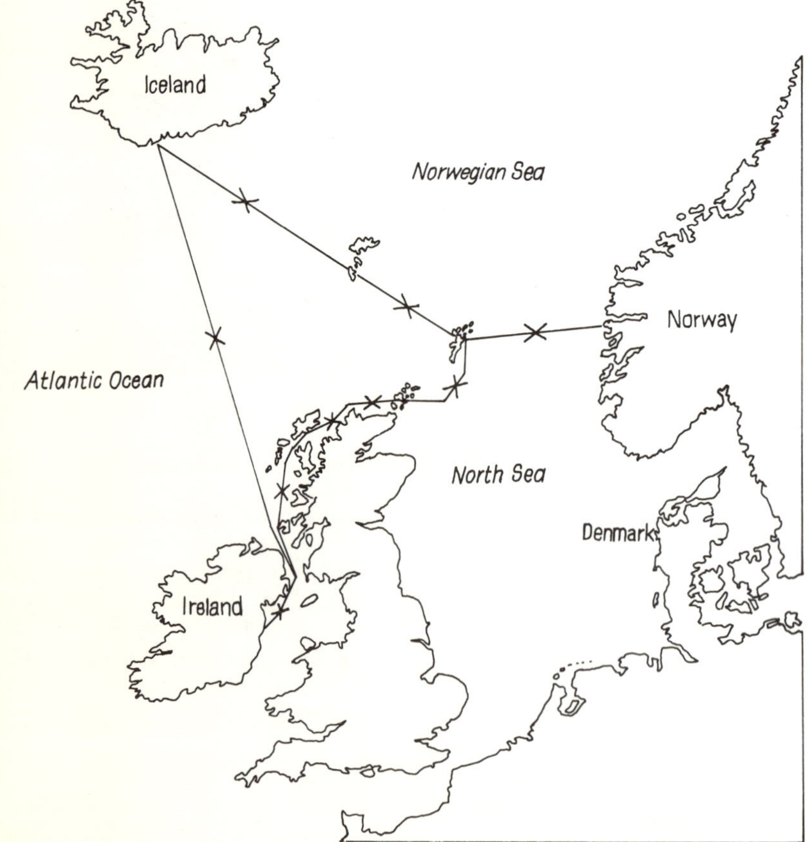

The remains of a ninth-century Viking building at Buckquoy in Orkney

If you look at the map of Scotland in the tenth century, (after 900 A.D.) when Constantine II was King you will see that the main groups of people in Scotland were under attack by the Vikings.

- Do you think they continued to fight each other?

The Vikings were also important for the trade they brought to Scotland. The Hebrides and the west coast of Scotland were very important here as they were on one of the main sea trade routes which led to the important market centre, Dublin.

Over the years, kings of Dublin, the kings of Man and kings of the Hebrides and other islands like Somerled of Argyll fought against each other to control this area.

- Do you think the Vikings thought of the Orkneys and the Hebrides as remote islands, as we do today?

For about four hundred years the Vikings controlled the Northern and Western islands of Scotland, but at the same time they began to mix with the local people. Some of the kings of Norway sometimes made great *expeditions* through the Northern Islands to show their strength.

Not long after the Vikings came to Scotland they became Christians. We know this from the changes in the way they were buried. Before they became Christians they put various weapons, *sacrificed* horses, and even boats into the graves. Later they were buried without these grave goods.

The Vikings were important in the "Making of Scotland", and the Northern Isles still show signs of their influence.

- Can you find out what signs there still are of the Vikings in the Northern Isles?

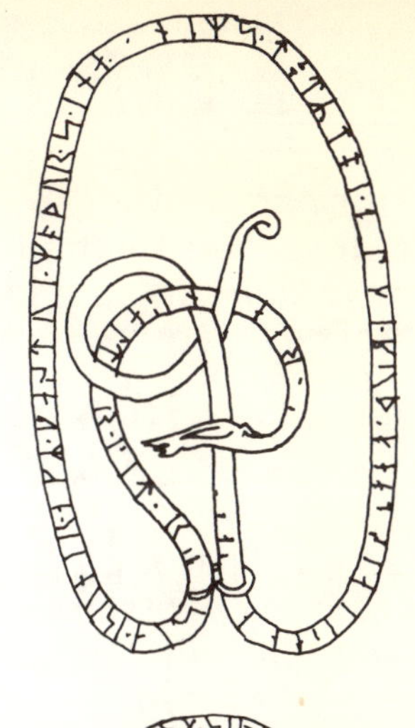

Runic inscriptions from Viking gravestones

More questions and assignments

1. Make a drawing of a Viking longboat. Now answer the following questions.
   a. What power did these boats use to move?
   b. How did the Vikings protect themselves from bad weather when they were on the ship? Say what *you* think.
   c. How many people do you think this boat carried?

2. From what you have learnt in this chapter write at least 5 lines to explain how we know that the Vikings were not just fighting warlike people.

3. On a map of Europe mark on the area the Vikings came from, then draw on arrows showing which way they went to Scotland and England. Put other arrows on the map to show where else they went to and name the places. You will need to use other books to find this information.

7 The Normans in Scotland

While the northern and western coasts and islands were still being taken over by the Norwegian Vikings, the Normans were beginning to spread out from their lands in northern France. They were *professional* soldiers in search of glory, land and wealth and they first came to Scotland in the eleventh century (after 1000 A.D.). By this time Scotland was ruled by one king, Macbeth, who was fighting to keep his throne with the help of those hired Norman soldiers. In 1040 A.D. he had killed King Duncan and taken the kingdom for himself; for seventeen years he ruled Scotland, but Duncan's son Malcolm took revenge for his father's death and Macbeth was killed.

Macbeth's Norman fighting men had done him no good, but soon the new king, Malcolm, and his successors would have to give way to them. In 1066 A.D. the Normans, led by their Duke William, landed in southern England and within a few weeks the English King Harold was defeated and dead and William and his followers took over the crown and the lands which had belonged to the English *nobles.* Malcolm tried to help the English to keep the Normans out of England and married Margaret, the sister of Edgar (who claimed to be the proper king of England after Harold was killed). Scotland was not conquered, but King William soon made the Scottish King Malcolm realise how powerful the Normans were. The part of the Anglo-Saxon Chronicle written after 1100 A.D. tells us that in 1072 A.D.:

Norman soldiers

King William led an army into Scotland and made war there. And King Malcolm came and made peace with King William and gave him *hostages* and promised to be King William's follower. Then William went home with his army.

● How did the Normans show King Malcolm how powerful they were?

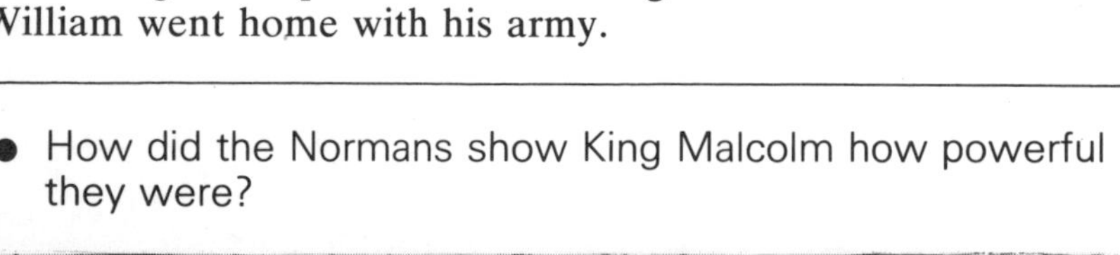

Part of the Bayeux tapestry showing some of the Norman soldiers who invaded England with William the Conqueror

But before there were many Normans in Scotland, changes had already begun. King Malcolm's new wife Margaret had travelled through Europe. When she came to Scotland she was determined to change the way of life at the court.

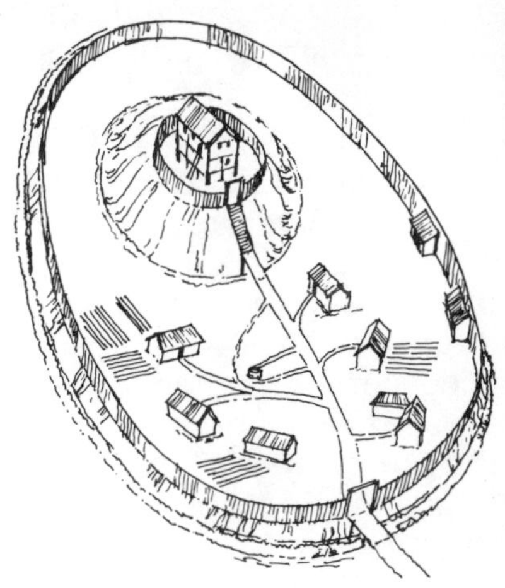

What a motte and bailey castle would probably have looked like

● What sort of changes do you think the Normans brought about?

Margaret, who was later made a saint, was very religious and did much work for the church in Scotland, helping to set up new monasteries and encouraging *pilgrimages* by paying for ferry boats across the Forth to carry the *pilgrims* on their way to the shrine of St. Andrew, who was made the *patron* saint of Scotland.

It was Queen Margaret who brought the first *Benedictine* monks to Scotland, to found the Abbey of Dunfermline. Florence of Worcester, who wrote a chronicle at the start of the twelfth century (after 1100 A.D.), says this about Margaret:

She was a devoted upholder of religion, justice, peace and charitable works. She prayed continually and often fasted. She made churches and monasteries rich and treated God's servants with great kindness. All pilgrims who visited her were provided with shelter, clothes and food.

Margaret meeting Malcolm Canmore

Dunfermline Abbey

King Malcolm and Queen Margaret spent much of their time in Dunfermline, but Edinburgh castle was another important royal palace. It was there that a chapel was built for Margaret in the style of the time, with rounded arches over the windows and doors and holding up the roof. The same style, usually called 'Norman', can be seen in other Scottish buildings of that time.

Margaret's husband, Malcolm Canmore, was King of Scots for 36 years — a very long time in those days when kings were often killed by rivals or died of ill-health at a much younger age than is usual now. During his reign he often supported those who rebelled against King William and his successors in England, hoping that if William could be defeated Scotland would be able to take over some of the lands of northern England. When Malcolm was fighting against the English King, William II, in 1093 A.D. he was killed in battle.

The next four years were troubled ones for Scotland as there was fighting between nobles who thought they should be king. This is described in a chronicle written at the time:

A Norman arch

When Malcolm and Margaret died the Scots chose Donald, Malcolm's brother, as King. Duncan, Malcolm's son, took the crown from Donald with the help of King William of England and was accepted as King as long as he promised to have no English or Norman advisers . . . A year later the Scots killed King Duncan and made his uncle, Donald, King for a second time . . . Three years later Edgar, son of Malcolm Canmore, with King William's help and after a great battle won the Kingdom from King Donald.

● Why do you think the Scots wanted Donald and not Duncan as their king?

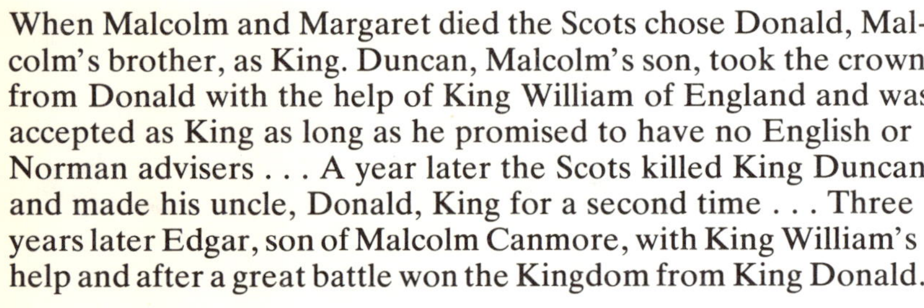
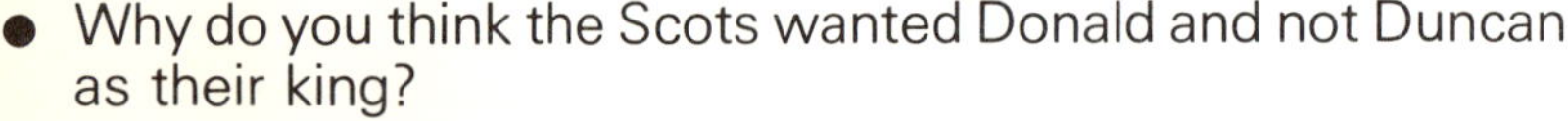
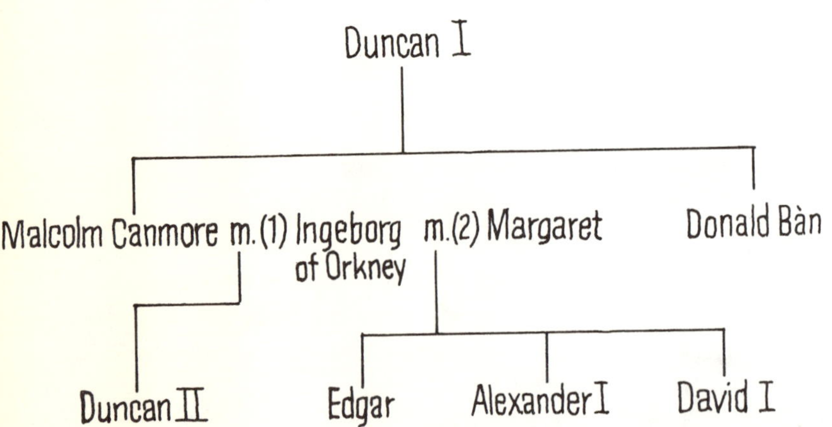

A family tree of Malcolm and Margaret showing the order in which their sons became kings of Scotland

The kings who came after Malcolm, Edgar and his brothers Alexander and David, took to Norman ways of living. They also organised their kingdom in the same way as England

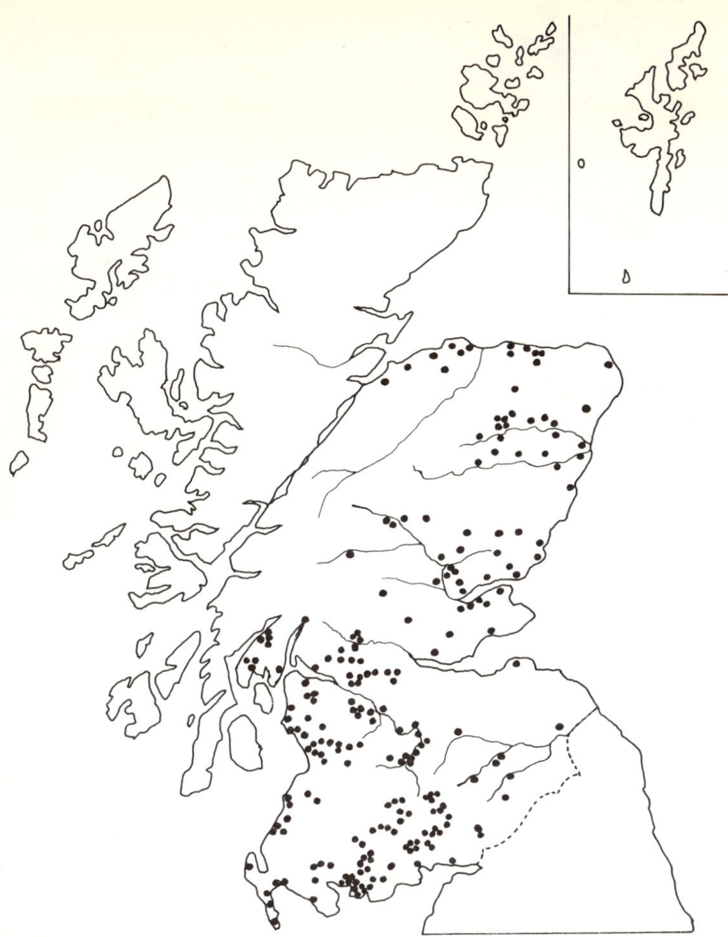

A map showing where motte and bailey castles were built

was being organised by her Norman kings. King David brought with him from England many Norman nobles and provided them with land in southern Scotland. They built *Motte and Bailey* castles like the one shown on page 39, and controlled the areas round their castles for the King, punishing lawbreakers, collecting taxes and raising an army to fight for the King when there was war. The King could not rule his land without these Norman lords and had to listen to their advice. Many of the King's new followers were given land in Galloway and Moray where there had often been rebellions. You can see from the map that there were many Motte and Bailey castles built in these areas.

● Why do you think so many Norman lords were given lands in Galloway and Moray?

This was a time of great changes in Scotland. Many of the Norman lords travelled between their estates in Scotland, England and France. They brought with them many new ideas and a way of life that was new to Scotland.

Before King David's time there had been no real towns in Scotland. Even Edinburgh was just a collection of a few

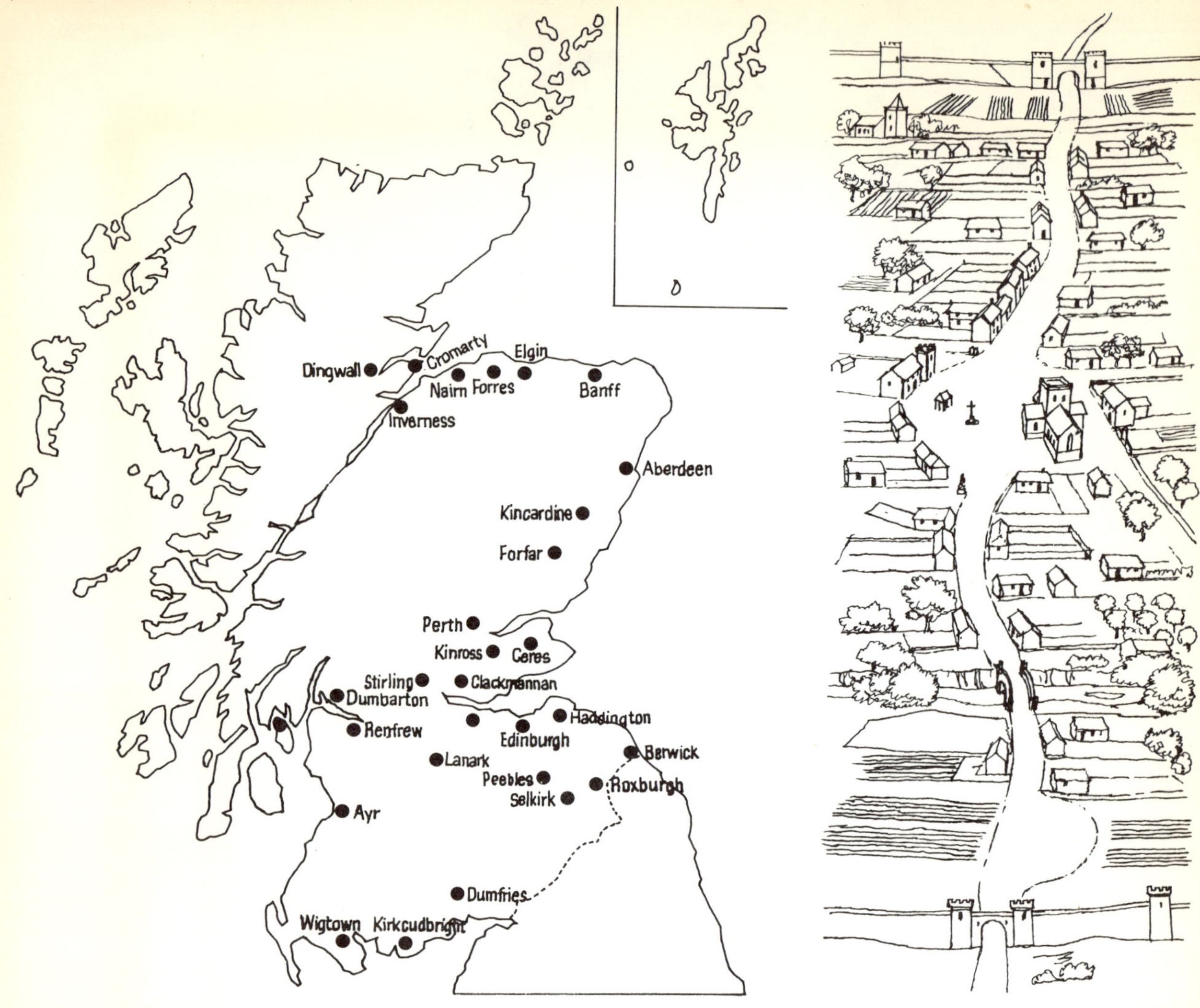

These are some of the main burghs (towns) in Scotland at the time of Alexander III

A drawing of what a burgh probably looked like

houses outside the gates of the *fortified* royal palace on the rock. But King David encouraged towns to grow in southern Scotland. These *burghs* were trading centres where foreign merchants could buy Scottish goods and sell luxury goods from abroad. Merchants were given their land and special trading *privileges* by the King. These privileges and conditions were written out in a *charter* by the King's *clerks*. Without a charter a burgh could not be started and only the King could give a charter.

Burghs were founded at places where roads met, or where a river was crossed by a bridge or where there was a good harbour.

● Why do you think burghs were founded in these places?

The kings of Scotland were never really strong enough to ignore the wishes of the kings of England. During David's reign, the Scots were badly defeated at the Battle of the Standard at Northallerton in northern England in 1138 A.D. Thirty-six years later the Scots were again beaten by the English and had to make a *humiliating* agreement called the *Treaty* of Falaise. Here is what it says:

William King of Scots has become the *liege man* of Henry King of the English. The King of Scots and all the important men of Scotland have done *homage* to the King of the English.

Fifteen years later when the English King Richard needed money for his crusade he agreed to release the Scots King from his promise in return for 10 000 merks (about £7 000). For the next hundred years England and Scotland seemed to be friends.

A man doing homage to his overlord

More questions and assignments

1. Imagine that you are a newspaper reporter who has travelled back through time to meet Queen Margaret. Write a report explaining what changes she brought to Scotland, and what kind of person she was.

2. Make a drawing of a woman dressed in the sort of clothes Queen Margaret would have worn.

3. Choose a Norman building and draw a doorway and a window — draw the decoration and patterns very carefully.

4. Using the maps on pages 41 and 42 draw a map of Scotland showing where most people lived in Scotland at that time.

5. Explain why towns grew up during and after King David's reign.

Many new peoples moved into different parts of Scotland over the centuries, but by the thirteenth century Scotland seemed to be settling down. There were no more invaders from overseas and peace was made with England.

The number of people living in the whole country in the thirteenth century (after 1200 A.D.) was only about 400 000 — less than the population of Edinburgh today. Most people lived in small villages with their land round about them. The ordinary people did not own land, but lived on land belonging to the lords, and the people themselves were the property of the lord who could sell them if he wished. If they left his land he could order them back. This is from a charter by King David I who ruled between 1124 and 1153 A.D.:

This drawing shows what a plough would have looked like in the thirteenth century

I command that all *serfs* who are the property of the Abbey of Dunfermline shall be sent back to the Abbey with all their belongings immediately. I forbid anyone to keep them from returning.

This is from another charter, written in 1258 A.D.:

I, Malise, Earl of Strathearn, for the *salvation* of my soul and the souls of my ancestors, have given to the abbot and monks of Inchaffray, John Starnes, son of Thomas and Thora, with all his children . . .

This drawing shows what the ordinary people probably wore in the thirteenth century

Below left: Peasants ploughing — this drawing is based on an illustration from a fourteenth-century prayer book

Peasants harvesting — women cutting the corn with sickles

The serfs worked for the lord and gave him a share of the crops they produced. In return they had land on which they could grow their own food. The land of the village was divided into long narrow fields called rigs and every family had several rigs. On the rigs they grew oats and barley. But in most areas the animals they kept were more important. The animals grazed on the open grasslands around the village, and each spring the animals were taken to the fresh pastures on the hillsides near the villages. The people ate simple food — barley, oatmeal, milk, cheese, fish and sometimes a little butter and meat. Their houses, clothing, furniture and tools

were also very simple and made by themselves. They did not use money, but exchanged things with each other — this is called *bartering.* Wood or peat was used for fires.

- Why do you think the lords wanted to keep the serfs in their power?
- Why did they move the animals to hillsides only in the spring?

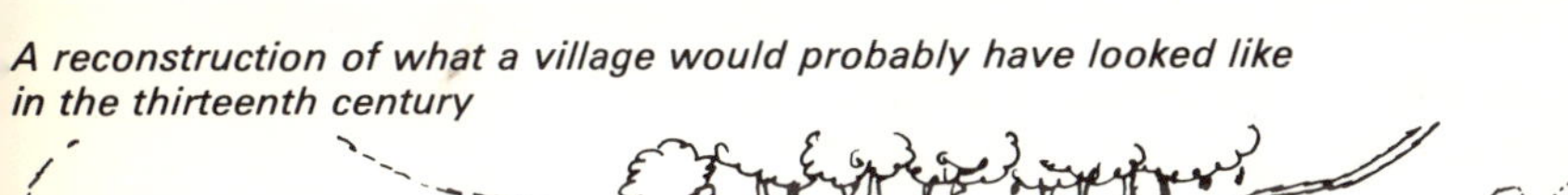

A reconstruction of what a village would probably have looked like in the thirteenth century

Apart from the rich and their servants and the merchants from the burghs, almost everyone made their living from farming. Even the monks, men who devoted their lives to God, spent much time working in their fields or looking after their flocks of sheep. Some monks also mined coal and collected salt, the only industries at that time.

Two documents (the first a charter by Malcolm IV written about 1160 A.D. and the second an entry from the *Register* of Newbattle Abbey about 1200 A.D.) tell us that the Abbey was given lands where salt and coal were found:

Let all men know that I, Malcolm King of Scots have given to God and the Abbey of Newbattle a saltpan at Callendar. I also give fuel from Callendar wood for making the salt.

Let all men know that I, Seyr de Quincy, earl of Winton, have given to God and the Abbey of Newbattle the coal workings and quarry between Pinkie and Inveresk . . .

Abbeys were often given gifts of land by the rich, especially by kings like David who founded many monasteries.

The monks lived according to the rule of St. Benedict which ordered them to live simple lives of poverty and hol-

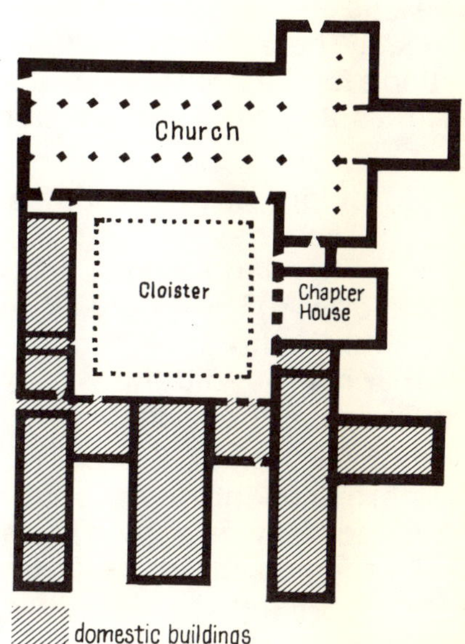

A plan of an abbey based on the thirteenth-century abbey at Dundrennan in Kirkcudbright

iness. But many of the monasteries were given so much land and wealth and were so successful in the business of selling the produce of their fields and the wool from their sheep that they became very rich. The monasteries became large and beautifully decorated places and they provided free food and shelter to pilgrims and travellers and cared for orphans, the sick, the old and the poor at a time when there were no hotels or hospitals.

Not all religious men were monks. Most priests lived among the ordinary people in the villages and often these priests grew their own food on land belonging to the church. In charge of the churches were men called bishops, who were usually from rich noble families. Each bishop controlled an area called a *diocese*, which was made up of many small parish churches each with its own priest. The bishop's own church was called a cathedral. There was one in each diocese in Scotland. In most countries an archbishop was in charge of the bishops, and at the head of the whole church was the pope in Rome. Scotland did not have an archbishop but the English archbishop of York claimed to be head of the church in Scotland. The Scottish bishops did not accept this.

● Look at the map which shows the areas controlled by bishops. Who controls all the Islands? Why is this?

The king and some of the nobles had hunting *reserves* called *forests*. There were laws to stop *poachers* and an official called a *forester* did the job of a gamekeeper looking after the animals and catching and punishing the law breakers.

For most people the law of Scotland was *administered* by the local lord or by the king's *official,* the sheriff, in the burghs (see map on page 42). There were sheriffs in most parts of Scotland who collected taxes and carried out the king's orders. The king was helped in ruling the country by the nobles who gave him advice. The priests, who could read and write, did the work of copying out the king's instructions and decisions.

In 1266 A.D. the King of Norway gave up his claims to western Scotland. In the south of the kingdom, the position of the border was agreed by the Scottish and English Kings and it seemed as if this was to be a 'Golden Age' of peace in which Scotland could trade with other countries and so become rich. But the English kings had not given up their

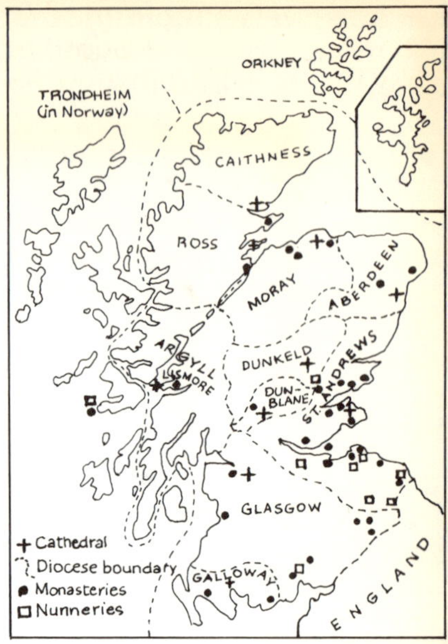

A map showing the areas controlled by bishops from the cathedral or chief church of the diocese

A drawing of the time which shows men hunting a stag

This map shows some of the royal 'forests' which were used by the king

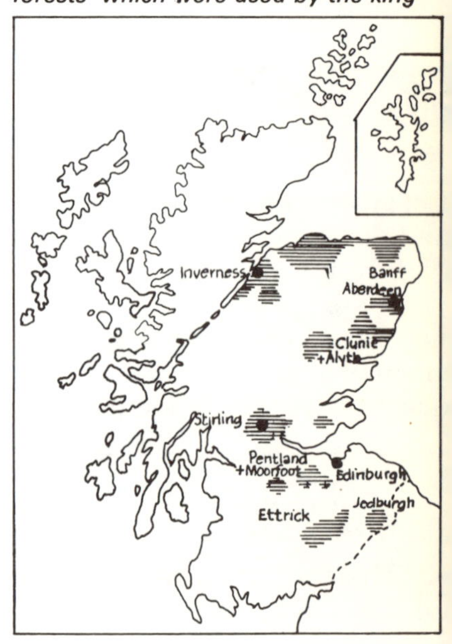

claim to be the *'overlords'* of the kings of Scotland. In 1278 A.D. Alexander III of Scotland was called to the palace of Edward I at Westminster to promise him obedience. Here is what a monk, writing at the time, tells us:

Alexander King of Scots said these words, "I have become your man for all the lands which I have in the Kingdom of England." One of the English bishops quickly said, "The King of England has a right to homage from your Kingdom of Scotland too." But Alexander replied in a loud voice so that everyone could hear him, "Only God has a right to homage for my Kingdom."

● Did King Alexander promise to obey King Edward I of England?

The English Church said that the Scottish Church should do as it was told by England, but Pope Honorius III said in 1218:

We most strictly forbid anyone to interfere in the affairs of the Scottish Church as it is under the power of the Pope as a special daughter.

● How did the Pope try to settle the quarrels between England and Scotland?

King Edward did not have long to wait for his chance to try to make the King of Scotland his *vassal.* Alexander III's two sons died before him and as his *heir* he had only a baby granddaughter, Margaret, Maid of Norway. The Scots lords had no choice but to promise to accept Margaret as the next Queen although she was only a child. If they did not accept her they knew there would be war between powerful nobles fighting for the throne.

Unfortunately for Scotland, Alexander died two years later and the new Queen Margaret died in the Orkney Islands on her way to Scotland. This gave King Edward his opportunity to interfere in Scotland again, and for the next twenty-five years the King of England tried to force the Scots to accept him as their overlord.

Part of the typical defences of a thirteenth-century castle

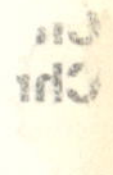

More questions and assignments

1 Describe one day in the life of the three following thirteenth-century people; a lord, a monk and a serf. Use the information in this book as well as your imagination.

2 Why did the kings of England and Scotland so often disagree, do you think? Write a few lines to explain this.

Glossary

Abbot — chief man in a monastery

A.D. — when this abbreviation appears after a date it means that the number of years are counted from the birth of Jesus
"Anno Domini" means "years after Christ"

Administer — to organise and see that things are done

Aerial Photography — a photograph taken from the air

Aligned — put in a straight line with something else

Analyse — see what something is made of

Archaeologist — someone who digs to find the remains of places where people lived long ago

Artifact — something made by hand

Barbarian — anyone who was not a Roman

Barter — to swop one thing for another; to buy without using money

B.C. — when this abbreviation appears after a date it means that the number of years are counted back from the birth of Jesus, so 100 years B.C. was longer ago than 50 years B.C. B.C. means "Before Christ"

Benedictine — describes a monastery or convent organised as St. Benedict ordered

Broch — a stone tower, 10-15 m. high, built for protection from attack

Bronze — a metal made by mixing copper and tin

Bull — a letter from the pope

Burgh — a town which has been given privileges and duties by the king

Campaign — a series of battles against the same enemy

Cereal — any kind of grain crop

Charter — a letter making a gift to someone

Chronicle — a history book written by monks and nuns which tells what happened each year

Clerk — someone who could read and write — almost always a priest or monk

Comet — a star with a tail

Communal — to do with the whole community or group

Contemporary — from the same time

Convert — to get someone to change from one religion to another

Craft — a special skill like pot-making

Craftsmen — people who had a special skill, like pot-making and who often earned their living by it

Crannog — a house on a man made island, built of stones, wood and earth, at some distance from the shore of a loch or river

Culdees — monks who sometimes lived in separate cells or huts. These cells were replaced by monasteries from the time of King David onwards

Diocese — the area ruled by a bishop

Dun — a fort with a wall built of stone

Empire — a kingdom which has grown and taken over other less powerful kingdoms

Evidence — clues as to what has happened

Excavate — to dig a place up

Expedition — a journey of exploration or conquest

Forest — lands in which only the king or some other important person was allowed to hunt — not always covered with trees

Forester — A man who had to make sure that nobody else hunted in the forest area

Fortified — protected by a wall and ditch so that it was difficult to attack

Frontier — the border of a country — where another country begins

Grave Goods — things put with the body of a dead person for the next life

Heathen — anyone who does not believe in God

Heir — the person who will inherit, or be given, the rights or property of someone else who dies

Homage — to give homage to someone is to say that you will take his orders

Hostage — someone kept prisoner to force another person to do something

Humiliate — to make a fool of someone

Hypocaust — a Roman heating system

Implement — a tool

Influence — the ability to change other people's ideas or customs

Kin — belonging to the same family

Landmark — a thing or place that can be seen from far away

Liege Man — someone who has promised to obey and respect someone who is more powerful and rich

Maraud — attack, destroy and rob

Metalworkers — people who use metal to make tools or weapons

Midden — rubbish dump

Migration — a group of people (or animals) leaving one land and going to live in another

Missionary — someone who spends his life spreading religious ideas

Motte and Bailey — a type of castle surrounded by a ditch and raised up on a mound of earth

Myth — a story from the past which we do not believe is true

Nobles — important men who owned lands and were called lords

Nomads — a group of people who continually move from place to place

Official — someone who is given the power to do a job for someone else